THE HEART THAT GREW THREE SIZES

The Heart That Grew Three Sizes:
Finding Faith in the Story of the Grinch

The Heart That Grew Three Sizes
978-1-7910-1732-3
978-1-7910-1733-0 eBook

The Heart That Grew Three Sizes: Leader Guide
978-1-7910-1734-7
978-1-7910-1735-4 eBook

The Heart That Grew Three Sizes: DVD
978-1-7910-1736-1

The Heart That Grew Three Sizes: Youth Study Book
978-1-7910-1741-5
978-1-7910-1742-2 eBook

The Heart That Grew Three Sizes: Children's Leader Guide
978-1-7910-1745-3

The Redemption of Scrooge: Worship Resources
978-1-7910-1743-9 Flash Drive
978-1-7910-1744-6 Download

Also by Matt Rawle
The Faith of a Mockingbird
The Salvation of Doctor Who
Hollywood Jesus
The Redemption of Scrooge
What Makes a Hero?
The Gift of the Nutcracker
The Grace of Les Miserables

With Magrey R. deVega, Ingrid McIntyre, and April Casperson
Almost Christmas

For more information, visit MattRawle.com.

MATT RAWLE

THE HEART
THAT GREW THREE SIZES

FINDING FAITH IN
THE STORY OF THE GRINCH

Abingdon Press / Nashville

The Heart That Grew Three Sizes:
Finding Faith in the Story of the Grinch

Library of Congress Control Number: 2021941507

978-1-7910-1732-3

21 22 23 24 25 26 27 28 29 30 — 10 9 8 7 6 5 4 3 2 1
MANUFACTURED IN THE UNITED STATES OF AMERICA

CONTENTS

INTRODUCTION

How the Grinch Stole Christmas! has remained an iconic story for several generations because of its seasonal theme, happy ending, universal ambiguity, and moral conclusion. The ambiguity throughout the story perpetuates an exciting mystery to the motivation behind both the Grinch's hatred of Christmas and his seemingly sudden transformation. We aren't quite sure why the Grinch is so miserable in the original story, which allows the readers to identify their own frustrations in the Grinch's character. Sometimes we are melancholy during Christmas season and it's difficult to understand precisely why. Whether we appreciate it or not, it's easy to identify with the Grinch's aggravation.

Likewise, at the end of the story we aren't given a reason why the Grinch's heart grew three sizes. It seems to be miraculous and immediate, which is precisely how many children might identify the feeling they have on Christmas morning. Children are quick to recognize the beauty of the story's ending as well. The Whos do not seek retribution or vengeance; rather they invite the Grinch to eat with them at the table. In other words, they become friends in the eating, which is certainly within children's hopeful imaginations.

Doctor Seuss purposefully did not make the Grinch overtly religious because he wanted the story to be more universal in tone. In fact, Seuss identified with the Grinch's frustration over the commercialization of Christmas, and soon began to realize that the Grinch's story was more autobiographical than he cared to admit. Since its publication, *How the Grinch Stole Christmas!* has been translated into nine different languages, adapted for television in 1966 with several subsequent movie adaptations, as well as being produced for the musical theater stage in 2007. The Grinch has become such an iconic character in our collective holiday imaginations that, beginning as early as 1966, the word *Grinch* was informally used as a synonym for "killjoy," officially being added to *Webster's Dictionary* roughly twenty years after the story's initial publication. The Grinch's story is universal in scope, easy to understand, and ends with a positive message of hope and reconciliation, which is why it continues to be such a powerful Christmas story today.

THE POP IN CULTURE

What comes to mind when you hear someone refer to *pop culture*?

Maybe you think about the latest playlist on Spotify or the new releases on Netflix or the top-grossing smartphone apps. Or maybe you think of something more under the radar. Sometimes pop culture begins with a small, fanatic fan base who loves a relatively unknown book, movie, band, or artist. Maybe there's the band you never hear on the radio but everyone's talking about. Or that series of novels you think looks weird but that inspires legions of people to write "fan fiction" surrounding its main characters. Sometimes, instead of becoming trendy, these artists retain a faithful insider following. They become less "pop" and more "cult," becoming what is known as a "cult classic."

Regardless of if you picture an example of "pop culture" as an innovative hit like *Breaking Bad* or something more fanatic and underground like *Firefly*, there's no denying that the popular music, books, television, movies, and media have much to say about the world in which we live. The word *culture* is used often, by many different people in many different ways; but in its simplest form, culture is simply an expression of how a community understands itself. God, our Creator, supplies us with the raw ingredients of humanity—talents, time, creativity, desires, ingenuity—and "culture" is whatever we cook up. Stories, songs, recipes, traditions, art, and language are all displays of how we interpret the world and our place in it.

So what role does God play in our culture—in our day-to-day lives and in the work of our hands, which produce music and art and literature and plays and movies and technology? Throughout history, people have debated this issue and adamantly drawn a dividing line between that which should be considered "sacred" (that which is explicitly religious in nature) and that which should be considered "secular" (that is, everything else). This is as true for our Christmas-themed music and stories as it is for everything else, perhaps more so. At first glance, these may be seemingly easy judgments to make, but when we stop to examine what God has to say about this division, we might be surprised at what we find.

Scripture says that *all* things were made through Christ (John 1:3), and through Christ all things were reconciled to God (Colossians 1:20). In other words, everything and everyone in our world contains a spark of the divine—everything is sacred, and whether or not we choose to live in that truth depends on our perspective. For example, think of sunlight as a holy (sacred) gift from God. God offers us sunlight so that we can see the world around us. We can celebrate the sacred by creating things that enhance the light in our homes, such as larger windows or skylights, or we can hang heavy drapes and close the shutters in order to diminish the sacred and shut out the light. Our sacred work is letting in as much light as possible, and those things that keep the light out need to be rejected or transformed.

Through Jesus, God put on flesh and walked among us, in our world, in order to re-narrate what it means to be a child of God. God assumed culture and transformed it. That is the very mystery of the Incarnation that we celebrate at Christmas and await during the Advent season. So now all is sacred, and in everything we are to see and proclaim his glory. I truly believe we are called not to reject the culture we live in, but to re-narrate its meaning—to tell

God's story in the midst of it. Jesus didn't reject the cross (the sin of our world); rather, Jesus accepted it and transformed it from a death instrument into a symbol of life and reconciliation.

Sometimes it's easy to see God in the midst of culture—in the stories of Scripture and in reverent hymns and worshipful icons. Other times the divine is more veiled—hidden in a novel, concealed in classic rock, obscured by an impressionist's palette, or buried in the heart of a Grinch that starts off two sizes too small. The Pop in Culture series is a collection of studies about faith and popular culture, designed to help us see God in works like these. Each study uses a work of pop culture as a way to examine questions and issues of the Christian faith. Our hope and prayer is that this study and others in the series will open our eyes to the spiritual truths that exist all around us in books, movies, music, and television.

As we walk with Christ, we discover the divine all around us, and in turn, the world invites us into a deeper picture of its Creator. Through this lens of God's redemption story, we are invited to look at culture in a new and inviting way. We are invited to dive into the realms of literature, art, and entertainment to explore and discover how God is working in and through us and in the world around us to tell God's great story of redemption and transformation.

A QUICK REFRESHER

How the Grinch Stole Christmas! by Theodore "Dr. Seuss" Geisel, is a children's Christmas story that follows a grouchy, miserable Grinch who lives in isolation above the town of Whoville. In the book, published by Random House in 1957, Seuss narrates what is now a Christmas classic detailing how the Grinch, so upset at the Whos' seasonal celebration, plots to steal away everything that has anything to do with Christmas. Although the story has been adapted several times for television, movies, and a musical, the basic story has remained relatively the same.

The Grinch lives alone on the top of Mt. Crumpit, with only his dog, Max, as a companion. Immediately we discover that the Grinch hates Christmas, which is probably because his heart is two sizes too small. Because the Grinch hates Christmas, he also despises the Whos and their Christmas celebration, which to the

Grinch is garish, noisy, and annoying. Whether to punish the Whos, or simply to spread his appreciation for misery, he decides on a "wonderful, awful idea" to steal Christmas away.

Donning a Santa suit, and riding a sleigh pulled by his reindeer-dressed dog Max, the Grinch sneaks into Whoville in the middle of the night on Christmas Eve to steal all of the presents, decorations, and Christmas food. When he arrives at the first house in Whoville the young Cindy Lou Who interrupts his thieving and asks him why he is taking everything away. Without hesitation the Grinch lies and tells the young child that he plans to fix the lights on the tree and will soon return it. After giving the child a glass of water, he sends her back to bed as he quickly finishes the job without interruption. The Grinch does the same with all the homes in Whoville before slinking back to Mt. Crumpit.

On the precipice of the mountain, the Grinch slowly begins to push all his gathered items off the edge of the cliff, destroying any hope that Christmas will arrive. He pauses momentarily as the Whos are waking up, hoping to hear the weeping and wailing he assumes will fill the air. To his astonishment the Whos begin singing. It seems that his plan didn't work. Even without the packages, food, and decorations, Christmas came anyway. After puzzling for three hours as to why his plan failed, his heart grew three sizes. He immediately returns the gifts to the joyfully singing Whos, and the story ends with the Grinch carving the roast beast at the head of the table.

CHAPTER ONE

WHEN EVERYTHING IS WRONG

When you hear or read the word *Grinch* what's the first thing that comes to mind? Do you think of that strange, green creature who lives on top of Mt. Crumpit? Do you hear Boris Karloff's deep bass voice describing the most miserable of beings? Maybe you're thinking of that person you just saw at Thanksgiving who never seems to be in the Christmas spirit. Maybe you're thinking about yourself. Whether you've read the original Dr. Seuss's *How the Grinch Stole Christmas!* as a bedtime story, gathered the family together to watch the television special, or hit the theaters for one of the movie adaptations, you know how this story never seems to leave our imagination.

When he originally published *How the Grinch Stole Christmas!* as a stand-alone story in 1957, Dr. Seuss set out to tell a Christmas story that pushed against the mainstream. He tried to avoid kitschy and sentimental moralisms, and in the process, developed a character synonymous with ill temper, mischief, and an irrational distaste for all things Christmas. Geisel quickly began to realize that his story was autobiographical. His personal disdain for sleigh bells, sappy music, and garish decorations was more than enough fodder for the Grinch to be endearing.

I love Christmas, but of course there are some parts of it that I don't like. Some of the songs, for example, are just terrible. One year I published a daily online survey of what I considered to be the worst Christmas songs of all time, and I invited people to vote in a tournament-style bracket to crown the winner. I specifically asked for people to vote for one song or the other without comment, but it didn't take long before people became curious as to why I selected the songs I did. To me it was obvious that "Little Drummer Boy," although not the winner, is one of the worst Christmas songs ever. I didn't see a need to explain that it's obnoxiously repetitive, never mind that the very last thing a new parent wants is for someone to start banging a drum just after they've placed the sleeping baby in a manger. Maybe you are just fine with all the holiday music, drumming and all, but you'd just as soon go without some of the food. We don't all have a deep personal aversion to Christmas like the Grinch does, but maybe we all have parts of the season that we dislike—and that is what allows us to identify with the Grinch.

Whatever we find in this story, it's undeniable that something about it speaks to many people. As you'll discover in this book, much of what resonates with us in the Grinch's story can help us understand our faith as Christians, the hope that we find in the birth of Jesus, and how God is calling us to respond to the inbreaking of God's kingdom.

IT'S THE MOST WONDERFUL TIME OF THE YEAR?

It's the most wonderful time of the year! When I hear these words I can't help but hear Andy Williams crooning over the radio singing about hosting parties, toasting marshmallows, and caroling out in the wintry weather. The Christmas he's describing sounds amazing, and for many of us, his description is correct. For me, Christmas is the most wonderful time of the year. People are more generous and kind, the music is festive and fun, and more so than any other time of the year, people share symbols and images of Christ.

With such joy and frivolity to go around, how could anyone not love the Christmas season? Maybe that's why the Grinch has captured our imagination for so many years. *How the Grinch Stole Christmas!* opens with a sad, miserable, red-eyed creature loitering about the opening of a dismal cave. His frown suggests that he's forgotten how to smile. The story tells us that the Grinch *hated* Christmas. The word is italicized for emphasis. The Grinch wasn't just having a bad day. It's not that he received an awkward present under the tree or somehow missed an invitation to the office Christmas party. He *hated* Christmas.

When reading this story to my kids, I always emphasize "hated." As if scripted, my kids invariably have the same response. Their eyes get big and their mouth turns down, as if they are in earshot to hear me yell "fiddlesticks" after stepping on a toy I've asked them to put away. The Grinch's hate for Christmas is unexpected and surprising, and immediately we're left wanting to know more.

When something is surprising or inexplicable, we often want to know why. Why do bad things happen to good people? Why do good things happen to bad people? Why does anything happen at all? We might think we remember why the Grinch hated Christmas, but actually we're never told. The title of Dr. Seuss's story is *How the Grinch Stole Christmas!* not "Why." Later adaptations of the story, such as the 2000 film starring Jim Carrey, explore the question of why with a back-story for the Grinch. But with the exception of a few theories about his head being screwed on wrong, his shoes being too tight, and his heart being too small, Dr. Seuss completely avoids the question over which we most hunger. Why?

It would make sense if the Grinch had a terrible Christmas memory, experienced loss, or had been ostracized by the seemingly joyous Whos, but maybe the story makes more sense if his reasons are left unknown. Suffering and hatred are complex realities, not equations with definitive answers. The story of the Grinch presents us with the fact of the Grinch's hatred as the story's beginning. In the same way, the season of Advent begins in the church not with joyous celebration, but with the reality of sin and suffering in our world. And like the Grinch's story, Advent does not rationalize sin or suffering, but simply names them as the starting point of the story, the things from which Jesus comes to redeem us.

The season of Advent, beginning four weeks prior to Christmas, starts with an unapologetic dive into suffering, and there is a strange tension between the words we hear from Scripture and the decorations we see. Every year before the first Sunday in Advent, our community gathers to decorate the sanctuary. We have five teams that separate to tackle a different area of our worship space. Those with a keen eye for visuals decorate the altar and table. The Silver Eagles, a group of retired men who know how to build and fix everything, put together the massive Chrismon tree. Several folks who aren't bothered by electricity wire the garland into the sconces along the walls. Our Hospitality Team decorates the narthex and gathering areas. Finally, the fifth team consists of folks who have foolishly finished their work too early and have been recruited to drape the chancel wall with endless spools of fabric.

On the first Sunday of Advent the congregation enters into a transformed sanctuary, with a beauty that echoes heavenly hosts singing about the Messiah's birth. But the Scripture reading of the day is not nearly as beautiful. There is despair and suffering, mourning and loss. The readings cry out for a messiah because destruction seems imminent:

> *O that you would tear open the heavens and come down,*
>   *so that the mountains would quake at your*
>   *presence—*
> *as when fire kindles brushwood*
>   *and the fire causes water to boil—*
> *to make your name known to your adversaries,*
>   *so that the nations might tremble at your presence!…*
> *We have all become like one who is unclean,*
>   *and all our righteous deeds are like a filthy cloth.*
> *We all fade like a leaf,*
>   *and our iniquities, like the wind, take us away.*
> *There is no one who calls on your name,*
>   *or attempts to take hold of you;*
> *for you have hidden your face from us,*
>   *and have delivered us into the hand of our iniquity.*
>   *(Isaiah 64:1-2, 6-7 NRSV)*

This reading certainly doesn't fit the lights, tree, garland, and bows. The author wants the Lord to make the divine presence known, but as the poem progresses, the author is no longer sure that the Lord's presence is a good thing. The mountains will tremble and the seas will boil, and it seems that it just might be our fault. Rather than hanging banners on the walls, we should have invested in an earthquake simulator.

Sometimes the changing of the season feels like the world is trembling, and sometimes it feels like it's our own fault. Maybe your annual Christmas tradition will need to be different this year. Maybe there isn't much room for gift-giving, and you know someone is going to be disappointed. Maybe there's some difficult news on the horizon, and you hope that you can just get through the holidays before letting the cat out of the bag. When these things happen, we can certainly feel like a "filthy cloth" or a leaf that is taken away on the wind. We might feel like, well, a Grinch, standing at the opening of an isolated, dark cave with nothing but a frown on our face. And as with the Grinch, there isn't always a "why." Your heart feels two sizes too small, and you can't figure out a reason. The decorations may be beautiful, the banners on the back wall larger than life, but when everything is going wrong, even our time-honored carols seem too loud and the lights on the tree too bright. Scripture reminds us over and over again that the Lord is near, but sometimes we may prefer to be on our mountain alone.

Are there some parts of the Christmas season that you don't like? What are they, and why don't you like them? How does it make you feel to see others finding joy in these aspects of the season?

Why do you think the story of the Grinch resonates with us?

Where do you see the reality of suffering in the world around you? Why is it important to acknowledge these realities at the beginning of Advent?

THE BEGINNING OF THE GRINCH

The Grinch character first appeared in a Dr. Seuss poem titled "The Hoobub and the Grinch" written for *Redbook Magazine* in May of 1955. The character was based on Dr. Seuss's own frustrations with the commercialization of the Christmas holiday, and his own sadness over his wife, Helen's, failing health. Seuss claimed that *How the Grinch Stole Christmas!* was the easiest story to write during his career with the exception of the ending. He said, "I got into a situation where I sounded like a second-rate preacher or some biblical truism.... Finally in desperation...without making any statement whatever, I showed the Grinch and the Whos together at the table."[1]

Green with Envy

Have you heard about the Mandela Effect? It's the phenomenon describing a false memory. For example, if you remember reading the Berenstein Bears as a child, you would be incorrect. That precious Bear family who taught many of us right from wrong spell their name "Berenstain." Or maybe you remember Mr. Monopoly and his monocle? Nope, his eyesight is perfectly fine. You might think you had a bowl of Fruit Loops this morning, but actually you poured milk over Froot Loops. Sometimes the false memory is a collective one, recalled by many people. The name "Mandela Effect," coined in 2010, comes from people collectively "remembering" Nelson Mandela's death in prison in the 1980s, when in fact he was still alive (Mandela died in 2013). In the spirit of things we think we remember, what color was the Grinch in the original Dr. Seuss story? If you said green, then you would be wrong. The original character had no color at all, save red eyes. The Grinch's iconic green fur was chosen for the television special that aired on CBS in 1966.

One of my favorite Christmas traditions is when my family would gather to recall stories from our childhood. One story in particular eventually became an inside joke within the family. Many years ago my sister woke up the household very early in the morning in a panic. She had to build a pueblo, a multistoried structure of the Pueblo people, for a school project that was due that morning, and she had totally forgotten about it. My mother quickly ran to Walmart to get the supplies, and the family hurriedly helped her finish the project just in time for the morning bell. Now, when anyone wakes up early in the morning panicked because of a forgotten deadline, we call it a "Pueblo Moment." This would be a great story, except it didn't happen. At least, it wasn't my sister who had to build the pueblo. It was me! For years I had believed that it was my sister who had alerted the house about the school project, until my entire family corrected me just a couple of years ago.

Advent is a time to prepare for the coming of Christ, and part of that preparation is to remember the story well. When the wise men followed the Bethlehem star and found themselves at Herod's palace, they inquired about where the new Messiah might be. Herod must not have remembered the story. He called the priests and scribes together to search the Scriptures because he didn't know them. They answered, "You, Bethlehem, land of Judah, / by no means are you least among the rulers of Judah, / because from you will come one who governs, / who will shepherd my people Israel" (Matthew 2:6). Maybe we should be thankful for Herod's forgetfulness, otherwise the Gospel of Matthew might be a much shorter read. Fear seized Herod when he heard that a new king had been born. If Herod had been looking for Jesus from the beginning, who knows how the story would have ended.

The point is not simply to remember, but to remember well. If Herod had well-remembered the Scriptures he would have known that this governor of Bethlehem would be the one who "will stand and shepherd his flock in the strength of the LORD . . . and he will become one of peace" (Micah 5:4a, 5a). This new governor would be far from a tyrant or overlord. Herod may have welcomed a successor who would unite all of Israel under the banner of peace, but power is a smokescreen to even the best of ideals. Herod became afraid, and all of Jerusalem with him. This is how tyrants work. The people of Israel knew that when an autocrat didn't have his way, it was the people who paid the price.

Why would good news of a peaceful-reigning king be met with such hostility? We might ask the Grinch the same question. He snarled at the Whos' stockings and growled at their greenery. The Grinch heard only noise when they sang their songs together. Maybe this is what Paul means when he writes that if we have not love we are "a clanging gong or a clashing cymbal" (1 Corinthians 13:1b). We may not know why the Grinch hated Christmas, but the Grinch's hatred warped his understanding and his memory of what Christmas was, just as Herod's fear and desire for power prevented him from seeing the birth of Jesus as good news.

When hate seeps into our thinking, it distorts our vision like a circus funhouse mirror or a bad Snapchat filter. Hate takes what is beautiful and makes it ugly.

When hate seeps into our thinking, it distorts our vision like a circus funhouse mirror or a bad Snapchat filter. Hate takes what is beautiful and makes it ugly. When I was in college, one of my friends and I weren't getting along. I can no longer remember why we were fighting, but the fight left a lasting effect. One of my favorite songs used to be "Bittersweet Symphony" by the Verve. The looping background string lick, the melancholy words, and the constant driving beat felt autobiographical when I was in college. It was my song, and I played it often. One weekend my friend, who happened to live next door, decided to go away for a few days. And because we were in a fight, he used it as an opportunity to make my life miserable. He cued up his CD player, turned the volume up as loud as it could go, and then set "Bittersweet Symphony" on repeat before locking his door and leaving. The song played nearly a thousand times before he returned. Not only that, the repeating string motif made it feel like the weekend lasted five hundred twenty-five thousand six hundred minutes. The only thing worse would have been if the repeated song was "Carol of the Bells."

Whatever we had been fighting about is long forgotten, but the song has been ruined forever. It may be a silly example, but that's what hate does. It takes what is beautiful, uses it as a weapon, and makes it ugly. It turns our good memories into bad ones. Christmas is beautiful. Christmas is profound. Pondering the mystery of Christ's birth is never exhausted, but the Grinch's hate for the Whos meant that the only solution that would satisfy his small heart would be to take what they love, use it as a weapon, and forever mar their memory. Hate had so distorted his experience of Christmas that he wanted to distort theirs to match. It's like creating his own Mandela Effect. He had hoped that the joyful music of the season might be remembered as a clashing, discordant cymbal. So, the Grinch developed a wonderful, awful idea.

Have you ever misremembered something? What happened, and how did you remember it? Why do you think you were mistaken in your recollection?

Why is it important to remember the Christmas story well?

How have you seen hate distort a memory or experience of something good?

A WONDERFUL, AWFUL IDEA

Do you hate anything? I'm not talking about rooting against North Carolina because Duke is the superior basketball team, or the exhaustion when your very talkative, distant family member has cornered you in the living room during Thanksgiving. I mean is there something that churns your stomach, raises your blood pressure, and consumes your thoughts with the mere mention of it? We might think that hate is a "bad word," but it's not without biblical precedent. God spoke through the prophet Amos against Israel's injustice and arrogance saying,

> *I hate, I reject your festivals,*
> > *I don't enjoy your joyous assemblies...*
> *Take away the noise of your songs;*
> > *I won't listen to the melody of your harps.*

But let justice roll down like waters,
and righteousness like an ever-flowing stream.
(Amos 5:21, 23-24)

Is it wrong to hate? Maybe it depends on what you hate. Through Amos, the LORD also says, "Hate evil, love good" (Amos 5:15a). It seems counter to the Christmas message to mention the word *hate*, but if we light candles of peace, hope, love, and joy, all that light is meant to dispel something. Lighting the candle of peace means we hate war. Shining a hopeful light means we hate despair's shade. A worshipful joy should stamp out our mourning, and the candle of love reminds us that "love should be shown without pretending. Hate evil, and hold on to what is good" (Romans 12:9).

I'm convinced that very few of us love evil and hate good. The problem is our definitions for good and evil can so often become confused. After being tricked by the wise men, King Herod ordered all the children two years and younger who lived near Bethlehem to be murdered. It seems that Herod believed his kingship and authority to be good, and anything that might challenge his authority to be evil. How could Herod possibly understand that what he was doing could have been good? We might ask the Grinch the same question. For the Grinch, Christmas is counter to everything he knows. He lives in isolation, he's never been invited to the party, and his heart is just not the right size to handle the peace, hope, love, and joy necessary to welcome the Christ Child.

I've often said that no one has a monopoly on meaning, that you can be wrong in your own understanding. Just before Jesus's

28

crucifixion Pilate asked Jesus about truth. Jesus said, "I was born and came into the world for this reason: to testify to the truth. Whoever accepts the truth listens to my voice" (John 18:37). The truth, the "good" of the good news is not a set of beliefs or doctrine; rather the truth is something to which you belong. So how do we know that we are in the truth? How do we know that our definition of *good* is good? "Whoever accepts the truth listens to my voice." Do we hear blessed are the poor? Do we hear love your neighbor? Do we hear love your enemies? Before we think that goodness is all puppy dogs and butterflies, do we also hear: "How terrible it will be for you legal experts and Pharisees! Hypocrites! You give to God a tenth of mint, dill, and cumin, but you forget about the more important matters of the Law: justice, peace, and faith" (Matthew 23:23).

How do we know that we are in the truth?
How do we know that our definition
of *good* is good?

So much of the Christian life is loving the right things, which also means setting aside or turning away the right things. It's an exercise in learning to love good and hate evil. Is our definition of good where it needs to be? And are our own Christmas traditions an exercise in choosing the good? The Grinch's distorted vision of Christmas, and his wonderful, awful idea, gives us an occasion to examine our own expectations of Christmas and the ways we celebrate.

GREEN FOR GRINCH

The iconic color green was not the Grinch's original color. In Dr. Seuss's original story, the only colors used were black, white, and red (with the Grinch having red eyes). The Grinch only became green with the 1966 animated television special, which well-represented his greedy and envious persona. After two months of storyboarding, Geisel (Dr. Seuss) and Chuck Jones (head of MGM Animation) finally landed on the color and design that set the tone for all subsequent Grinch adaptations including green fur, red eyes, and a grin that stretches from ear to ear.[2]

Does it make you uncomfortable to think of our faith instructing us to hate certain things, as in Amos 5:15 and Romans 12:9? Why or why not?

How can we be sure that we love the right things—that our definitions of good and evil are sound?

UNMET EXPECTATIONS

When the weather starts to turn colder, the music on the radio station changes, and my neighbors start to put lights on their homes, I have this almost giddy excitement. I always have in my head that *this* Christmas is going to be the best Christmas ever. I am certain that the kids will be overwhelmed with joy over the gifts they receive. My congregation will fill the pews and be so exuberant that the sanctuary will be just as full come the next Sunday.

Why do I do this to myself? I'm not expecting my children to tear their garments, weep with joy, and start building a shrine for me, but often Christmas morning feels a bit underwhelming. I'm not expecting to have three thousand baptisms on the Sunday after Christmas but having to keep the Christmas Eve folding chairs out would be a problem I'd be happy to have. I am always excited when the kids get out of school for winter break. I picture sleeping late, having quality family time together, and quick day trips to tree farms and holiday light displays. It isn't long before we start looking at the calendar to see when they will be returning to school.

Have you ever experienced unmet expectations? Was it because your expectations were too extravagant? Could it be that someone was underwhelmed? Maybe what you envisioned was embarrassingly off the mark?

The Grinch, too, experiences unmet expectations. And, as it turns out, these unmet expectations were the thing that could have happened. The Grinch assumes that stealing away what he thinks is Christmas will stop Christmas from happening. After returning from his midnight masquerading, he waits on Mt. Crumpit for the weeping and wailing he feels certain will happen. He leans in to hear a sound coming from Whoville, but instead of wailing he hears singing. He is surprised. Why didn't his plan work? He did exactly what he set out to do, and yet the outcome, thankfully, fell short of his expectations.

We have an amazing ministry in our congregation called "Downtown Friends," where each Saturday we offer food, clothing, and essentials to the homeless community in downtown Shreveport. One Saturday I took my two oldest daughters to help gift warm clothing to our downtown friends. On our way home I told my daughters how proud I was that they were there to help the homeless. Annaleigh said, "Wait...they were homeless? But they were so nice."

First, this reminds me of when the man and woman were in the garden. After eating the forbidden fruit they were hiding from God, so God called out to them—Where are you? "I heard that you were coming and I became afraid because I was naked, so I hid myself." God's first response is profound. God didn't say, you should be ashamed, or why are you clothed, or you should never hide from me. God said, "Who told you that you were naked?" Who told you that you were naked? Who told you that you should be ashamed? Who told you that you should hide? I responded to my daughter, "Who told you that homeless people weren't nice?" One of the great blessings of being a parent is when you experience when the lines are being blurred in your child's own discoveries. Whether it was learned or assumed, the lines of the box she had built to understand the world were being broken down, and it was beautiful.

But then she asked a question that started to dismantle my own assumptions and expectations. She asked me why they were homeless. I replied, "Well, it's complex. Sometimes it's because you've lost your job and you can't afford a home anymore. Sometimes people are ill and they can't keep a home . . ." But, to my embarrassment, she wasn't asking about what had gone wrong for those who are homeless. She was asking what was wrong with those of us who aren't homeless. "Why don't we build them a shelter and charge only one dollar a week? Why do we help them only on Saturdays? Why don't we do more to make a difference for them?" Her question, "Why were they homeless?" wasn't about the homeless. It was about us. It may be easy to dismiss such questions by saying that a child doesn't know how the world works, but the Christmas story is a story about how God seems unconcerned about our expectations.

*In the sixth month the angel Gabriel was sent by
God to a town in Galilee called Nazareth, to a virgin
engaged to a man whose name was Joseph, of the house
of David. The virgin's name was Mary. And he came
to her and said, "Greetings, favored one! The Lord is
with you." But she was much perplexed by his words
and pondered what sort of greeting this might be.*
(Luke 1:26-29 NRSV)

Gabriel's announcement went against Mary's expectation. She
asks, "How can this be because I am a virgin?" (verse 34). There
are several ways of reading this question. On the one hand this
could be Mary questioning the biology of it all, but there is also
this echoing of the prophet Jeremiah:

Now the word of the LORD came to me saying,

> *"Before I formed you in the womb I knew you,*
> *and before you were born I consecrated you;*
> *I appointed you a prophet to the nations."*

*Then I said, "Ah, Lord GOD! Truly I do not know
how to speak, for I am only a boy." But the LORD said
to me,*

> *"Do not say, 'I am only a boy';*
> *for you shall go to all to whom I send you,*
> *and you shall speak whatever I command you.*
> *Do not be afraid of them,*
> *for I am with you to deliver you,*
> *   says the LORD."*

Then the LORD put out his hand and touched my
mouth; and the LORD said to me,

> *"Now I have put my words in your mouth*
> *See, today I appoint you over nations and over*
> *kingdoms,*
> *to pluck up and to pull down,*
> *to destroy and to overthrow,*
> *to build and to plant."*
> *(Jeremiah 1:4-10 NRSV)*

Mary again echoes Jeremiah after she travels to meet her cousin Elizabeth who is pregnant with John the Baptist saying,

> *"He has shown strength with his arm;*
> *he has scattered the proud in the thoughts of their*
> *hearts.*
> *He has brought down the powerful from their thrones,*
> *and lifted up the lowly;*
> *he has filled the hungry with good things,*
> *and sent the rich away empty."*
> *(Luke 1:51-53 NRSV)*

The Grinch helps us see the need to evaluate our own expectations of the coming of Christ. This incarnate Word is God setting the world on its head, and we celebrate these words from Mary that finally we will be lifted up and we will be filled with good things. And then a young girl asks us, "Daddy, why are they homeless?" and then you realize that it is I who needs to be scattered and brought down and sent away. We never assume that we just might be Rome in the story. We never assume that we might be the Pharisee being rebuked.

Unmet expectations are sometimes the very thing we need.

At the same time, the Grinch shows us that unmet expectations are sometimes the very thing we need. The birth of God's Son to a poor Galilean woman was not what anybody expected. Her laying him in a manger was not expected either. And yet the manger is the throne of God, and it is disarming. We hear that the Messiah will be the Lord of lords, the Prince of Peace and he shall reign for ever and ever...and then like the shepherds we find a child wrapped in swaddling clothes and are amazed and totally disarmed. Stanley Hauerwas writes, "To be human is to be vulnerable, but to be a baby is to be vulnerable in a manner we spend a lifetime denying."[3] That's the thing about love. Love reveals when pride has gotten the best of us, love humbles us, love shows us where our expectations are all wrong. But love never tires of making sure that we are valued and that we are precious and that we are God's own.

What expectations do you find yourself having each year when Christmas rolls around?

What feelings might we have when our expectations are not met? How do those feelings affect our relationships with other people?

In what ways does Christ's birth upend your expectations?

WHEN THERE IS NO PEACE

At the end of the Christian year we meditate on the hope of everlasting life with All Saints Sunday, and the coming reign of Christ with Christ the King Sunday. On the first Sunday of Advent we are offered the grace to gather and tell the whole story again. Advent is a time of preparation to get ready to welcome the Christ Child into the world. One of the ways we prepare for Christ's arrival is to fill the world with symbols of our faith.

One of the first things I notice about the changing of the season is Christmas lights that start to adorn the houses in my neighborhood. It reminds me of the light the wise men followed while searching for Christ. Light illuminated their path. I think talking about Christ as the light of the world is almost as perfect as a metaphor can be. First, light is timeless. Light doesn't age or decay. The light that first began to glow shortly after the birth of the universe, if unimpeded, will travel across the cosmos until the universe ceases to be. When Revelation records that Christ is the Alpha and Omega, that is truth. Light was at the beginning, and it will be at the ending. The universe is so prodigally vast, that there is light so far away that we will never see it.

Secondly, light is powerful. One fall we lost power during a hurricane, and the sun began to set. My kids became nervous, so we lit a candle. A single candle can dispel darkness and consequently fear, if we allow it. Light is powerful, but also passive.

The point of light isn't to stare directly at it. Light illuminates everything but itself. If you stare directly at light, you become blind. The star was showing the wise men where Christ was, so that they might worship him, but Herod was blinded by its light, and therefore was afraid. If Herod had allowed the light to illuminate his path instead of illuminate himself, he would have known where Christ was.

But Herod couldn't look past himself and his own power. He became afraid, and Scripture says, all of Jerusalem became afraid as well. You see, when an autocrat becomes afraid of losing his power, he would rather see the entire nation and its people burn before stepping down peacefully. Christ is the light of the world because Christ is powerful. As we continue hearing this story we will hear about Christ's healings and miracles and profound teachings with authority. Christ is also passive in the sense that Christ was always pointing us toward God. Christ did not come to be an earthly king. For "God so loved the world that he gave his only Son, so that everyone who believes in him won't perish but will have eternal life. God didn't send his Son into the world to judge the world, but that the world might be saved through him" (John 3:16-17). This light was sent for us and for all of creation.

Third, light can also be used to communicate. Fiber Optic Cables, Morse Code, or my personal favorite, "Light the beacons of Gondor, so that Rohan will come to our aid"[4] When the wise men worshiped the Christ Child something was communicated to them that saved their lives. Scripture says that they had a dream or a vision or a revelation that they should travel home on a different path. Isn't it always the goal that when we commune with

Christ that we leave our gathering on a different trajectory that sends us where we need to be? Christ is the Word of God. Christ reveals the reality and the will of God.

Christ is the light of the world because Christ is our eternal and constant guide. Christ is the light of the world because Christ is powerful and passive. Christ is the light of the world because Christ communicates the reality and will of God. If we stare only at the light and forget that the light is meant for us to see one another and the world more clearly, then we will become blind. We will think that worshipping Christ is about power. We will think that being a Christian means that we are smarter, faster, more athletic. We will think that wise men from the east, because they are not from our own country, are a threat.

What does our life communicate about God, and what are the distorted things about our life that need redeeming? When we find peace with ourself, we will begin to find peace with one another.

This light offers peace. It offers a different path if we will allow it to show us the way. This peace begins with being at peace with ourselves. Love your neighbor as yourself. If you can't love yourself, it will be very difficult for you to love someone else. It's like a Grinch who is so distorted by his own hatred that he's unable to see Christmas for what it is. What does our life communicate about God, and what are the distorted things about our life that need redeeming? When we find peace with ourself, we will begin to find peace with one another. As we will hear on Christmas Eve, the angel proclaims—"Glory to God in the highest heaven, / and on earth peace among those whom he favors!" (Luke 2:14).

What does light symbolize for you?

What does your life communicate to others about God?

CHAPTER TWO

WHEN CHRISTMAS ISN'T CHRISTMAS

One of my favorite songs during the holiday season when I was young was "The Twelve Yats of Christmas," by Benny Grunch and the Bunch. It was a parody of "The Twelve Days of Christmas," which highlighted local New Orleans cuisine and landmarks. Instead of singing about ten lords a leaping, you sang, "Tenneco Chalmette Refinery." Instead of seven swans a swimming, you celebrated the "Seventeenth Street Canal." It was a fun way to celebrate our local culture during the holiday season, but it certainly wasn't something you would find in a hymnal. It sounded like Christmas. You could only hear the song on the radio during the Advent and Christmas season. But it wasn't Christmas.

A parody is a stylized imitation of something generally recognized. Think of how *Monty Python and the Holy Grail* is a stylized retelling of the King Arthur myth. Sometimes parodies can be great fun, like Weird Al Yankovik's music. Other times parodies are like a subversive language, communicating an important truth in a hidden, comical, socially acceptable way. The Book of Jonah can be read as a subversive parody of the Old Testament's prophetic tradition. God sends Jonah on a mission to preach to the people of Nineveh, but Jonah decides to go the other direction in a boat, thinking that God wouldn't find out. After Jonah is thrown overboard, wanting to die rather than do what God was commanding, a large fish saves him. Jonah gives thanks for God's salvation, and the fish vomits him up on the shore. Jonah goes to Nineveh and pathetically offers the shortest prophecy recording in the entirety of the Bible . . . and it works! All of the Ninevites repent from their wrongdoing, and Jonah who was praising God for his saving ways becomes angry that God also saves his enemy.

Grace is the greatest gift when it's offered to us, but it is the toughest pill in the world to swallow when it's offered to someone we don't think deserves it.

Jonah is an absurd story that nearly leaves us laughing out loud, but it also points us to the absurdity that sometimes we are angry with God's grace. Grace is the greatest gift when it's offered to us, but it is the toughest pill in the world to swallow when it's offered to someone we don't think deserves it. In this case, parody isn't poking fun at the prophets; rather it is subversively pointing at us.

This kind of subversive parody lies at the heart of the Grinch's wonderful, awful idea. The Grinch decides to take the marks of Christmas—Santa suit, reindeer and sleigh, bag full of toys, sneaking into the house in the middle of the night through the chimney—and turn them all on their head. He wears the Santa suit, but isn't a jolly gift-giver. The sleigh is powered by his dog, Max, rather than by flying reindeer. The sack that normally carries children's toys is used to steal them away. The Grinch uses all of the things he hates about Christmas against the Whos, almost as if he is an undercover spy infiltrating the system in order to sabotage it.

This is masterful storytelling. The Grinch, as a character, is treating things like Santa's suit and sleigh bells as the very things that make Christmas what it is and using them for a nefarious purpose. Dr. Seuss, on the other hand, is revealing that the decorations and the traditional cold weather symbols we easily associate with Christ's birth aren't what Christmas is all about. He's already given the punchline before the end of the story! The reason the Grinch is so easily able to misuse the Santa suit is because the Santa suit isn't the heart of the Advent and Christmas season. For example, if someone stole every copy of the sheet music for "Silent Night" in order to stop people from singing, it wouldn't work. The printed music helps us to learn and communicate "Silent Night," but it is not the music itself. Gifts under the tree, stockings hung by the fireplace, and a home adorned with ornaments and lights all have the potential to point us to the story of Christ's birth, but these cultural markers aren't the miracle itself. This is where the Grinch gets its wrong, and Dr. Seuss cleverly gets it right.

When King Herod heard about Jesus's birth, he called the wise men together and said, "Go and search carefully for the child. When you've found him, report to me so that I may also go and honor him" (Matthew 2:8). Herod is saying all of the right things, but he certainly isn't interested in offering gold, frankincense, and myrrh. It's like when the devil tempted Jesus in the wilderness at the beginning of Jesus's ministry saying, "[God] will command [his] angels concerning you, and they will take you up in their hands so that you won't hit your foot on a stone" (Matthew 4:6). That may be true, but Jesus rebukes the devil saying, "Don't test the Lord your God" (Matthew 4:7). Near the end of Jesus's life, the high priest Caiaphas said, "You don't see that it is better for you that one man die for the people rather than the whole nation be destroyed" (John 11:50). Caiaphas was looking for a reason to crucify Jesus in order to protect his own power. The words Caiaphas said weren't wrong, but sacrificial love, reconciliation with God, and the resurrected Jesus as the first fruit of God's victory over death were not what Caiaphas had in mind. Just like the Grinch, Herod, the devil, and Caiaphas looked and sounded the right way on the outside, but inside had a fundamental misunderstanding of the true meaning of Jesus and the story of his birth.

In the previous chapter, we began to meditate on the nature of peace. Peace can be a tricky thing. It's very easy to parody, easy to have something that looks like peace on the outside, but which is fundamentally a distortion of peace at its core. True peace is not a lack of conflict or the absence of war. That kind of peace was a means of control for Herod, the devil, and Caiaphas, and it was enforced by the threat of violence. It's true that people may think twice about stepping out of line under Herod's rule, but this also means that oppression, captivity, and turning a blind eye toward evil is the rule of the day. Jesus's birth is God's in-breaking into creation to "preach good news to the poor...release to the prisoners and recovery of sight to the blind, to liberate the oppressed" (Luke 4:18b). When Jesus's mother, Mary, meets her cousin Elizabeth, Mary proclaims:

> *[H]e has scattered the proud in the thoughts of*
> *their hearts.*
> *He has brought down the powerful from their*
> *thrones,*
> *and lifted up the lowly;*
> *he has filled the hungry with good things,*
> *and sent the rich away empty.*
> *(Luke 1:51b-53 NRSV)*

According to Isaiah, the coming Messiah will be known as the "Prince of Peace" (Isaiah 9:6). The peace that Jesus offers is neither parody nor absurd. This peace is not a means of control or oppression, celebrated because there is no conflict. This holy peace is a true reconciliation between God and humanity, and neighbor to neighbor. It is being at peace with one's self even when all the toys have been put away and the decorations removed. That is the kind of peace that Jesus comes to bring, and it goes far deeper and involves far more than the usual trappings of the Christmas season. This kind of peace is something the Grinch cannot steal.

What are some movies, books, songs, or parodies that remind you of Christmas, even though they may have little to do with the Christmas story?

If the Grinch were looking down on your household during the holidays, what do you think he would consider most important to you?

What is the difference between the peace that Christ brings and peace that comes through the rule of Herod and the Romans?

LOOKING THE PART

I've often joked that a Christmas song isn't a Christmas song unless there are sleigh bells in the band. There's something very Pavlovian about hearing sleigh bells over the radio as soon as Halloween is over. The same holds true with red and green decorations, gingerbread cookies, and giant socks hung in window displays. The Advent and Christmas seasons have a definitive look, smell, and taste. The lights we put on our homes, hearing the orchestra play "Sleigh Ride," and the gingerbread latte temporarily appearing on the Starbucks menu really don't have anything to do with Jesus's birth, but it hardly feels like Christmas until we sing, "Snow had fallen, snow on snow on snow," from "In the Bleak Midwinter."

One day I overheard Hillsong's "Seasons," on their *Christmas: The Peace Project* album playing in the background. One of the lyrics caught me off guard. I heard, "Lord I think of your love like the long winter sun," but "long winter sun" didn't make any sense. The whole reason it's cold during the winter season is because of a short winter sun. To make matters more confusing, Hillsong is out of Australia, and it's warm there during the Christmas season.

I had never really pondered how so many of the songs that we associate with Christmas have to do with wintry weather, and how songs about letting it snow and how cold it is outside really don't translate to the southern hemisphere. It's not even that Australia has a warm winter; December through March is actually called summer for half of the globe! My, how we assume that we are the center of the universe. With that said, the lyric was still confusing. Whenever winter happens, it's defined by short days, less sunlight than summer. How then can you have a long winter sun? Come to find out I had misheard the lyric. The actual lyric of the song is, "Lord I think of your love like the *low* winter sun" (emphasis mine), meaning that God's love grows even in winter to bring about the springing forth of life.

47

After laughing at myself for longer than a sane person should, I realized this still didn't solve the problem. Why would Hillsong sing a Christmas song rooted in winter that doesn't fit their own experience, where Christmas happens in summer? I realized that Hillsong was writing to fit their market rather than their local context. At the very least, it seems that warm weather Christmas songs aren't very popular. In fairness I wonder how often my own local congregation crafts mission and ministry for a market rather than a context. In other words, how often do we present what we want to see; rather than be about the work of what our people need? How often do we focus on getting the outward appearance of Christmas right, instead of truly anticipating and welcoming the presence of God with us?

How often do we focus on getting the outward appearance of Christmas right, instead of truly anticipating and welcoming the presence of God with us?

Sometimes we think that the Grinch is the bad guy in our story, and on the whole I think that's correct, but the fuss that the Whos make over Christmas isn't without some criticism. Maybe the Grinch is right in his aggravation over the grandiose decorations, the seemingly gluttonous eating, and the never-ending singing. When the Grinch stands outside of his cave on Mt. Crumpit, he isn't bothered that the Whos are expressing their faith or reaching out in concern and service in thanksgiving for

God's gift of the Christ Child. He's uptight about their mistletoe wreaths, noisy toys, never-ending feasting, and incessant singing, and it's hard to blame him.

In 2020, we had to make some pretty big decisions about how we celebrated Christmas. Normally, we would host concerts and Nativity pageants, large church dinners and hymns sung by candlelight. While we were planning our Advent and Christmas worship services, our area had reported thousands of COVID-19 cases every day, and there was little hint that anything was going to change. In response, we were facing a clear need to celebrate Christmas differently. Although we were still planning to worship together in person, congregational singing would be suspended, face coverings were mandatory, and physical distancing was in effect. I wasn't quite sure that Christmas would feel like Christmas, for lack of a more profound pondering. I literally did research on whether or not N-95 face masks were fire retardant. Could you imagine the horror?

In a way it did feel like the Grinch had stolen away many of the images and symbols we associate with Christmas, and maybe there's some truth to the Grinch's idea. We did end up offering a traditional service with many of the recognizable marks of Christmas Eve, but we also decided to do something new. We decided to bring our worship outdoors. We gathered together several fire pits out in the field behind our sanctuary. I grabbed my guitar, offered a simple message, and we gave thanks for Christ's birth. It was beautiful. It was simple. We didn't even pass the offering plate. Can you imagine not passing the offering plate on Christmas Eve? Knowing that we had missed our Easter offering

SEUSSIAN LATIN

Geisel wrote the songs for the 1966 television special himself, delighting in the opportunity to add something to one of his projects that a story can't offer. In the process, Geisel invented what he called "Seussian Latin." This fictional language in the opening song, "Welcome Christmas," began as "Dah Who Deeno," then became "Noo Who Fobus," until Geisel finally landed on Fahoofores, Dahoodores and the final refrain saying, "[It] seems to have as much authenticity as 'Adeste Fideles' to those untutored in Latin."[1]

early in the year because of stay-at-home orders gave me great pause to also miss our Christmas Eve collection. And even without the usual practices, Christmas Eve had never felt so authentic.

When we look at Jesus's birth in Luke's Gospel we notice that most of the glorifying and praising of God's gift happens outdoors. Luke makes a point to show us that the birth announcement did not happen in a palace. There was no room in the inn. Shepherds who were keeping watch over their flock by night were in the perfect place to notice angels in the evening sky. I fear that within our own sanctuary we might miss such a glorious wonder. Could it be that our guitar-driven anthems and carefully crafted worship backgrounds drown out the angels' proclamation happening against a star-studded canopy? At least I wonder how we might react if our "Silent Night" singing was interrupted by shepherds desperately seeking our attention to "tell all that they had heard."

What if God is even working through one whose heart is two sizes too small? What if it's been our heart all along that needed to grow?

Living through such a crisis makes quick work of discerning what is essential and what is not. As much as we love to hate the Grinch, maybe there is goodness we can glean from his aggravation. This year, with the COVID-19 pandemic and restrictions lessening in many parts of the U.S., will we be quick to go back to the pomp and circumstance of years past? The organ is certainly beautiful. Seeing the children fumble in period costumes at the Christmas pageant does bring in lots of parents we don't normally see throughout the year. Passing the bronze collection plate for end of the year giving does make the finance team meeting in January much more palatable. But what if not everything needs to be restored? What if God is even working through one whose heart is two sizes too small? What if it's been our heart all along that needed to grow through the simplicity and beauty of gathering around a fire under the midnight sky to give thanks and praise for the one who emptied himself so that we might know the radical love of God?

What is the most important or most meaningful part of the Christmas season for you? What do you do to celebrate Christ's birth?

Think back to your celebration of Christmas in 2020, during the coronavirus pandemic. What did you have to do differently?

How do we determine what is essential and what is not in how we celebrate Christmas?

SLEIGH BELLS

Every year a familiar controversy erupts on whether or not *Die Hard* is a Christmas movie. It takes place during Christmas, Christmas songs are found throughout the soundtrack, and it snows at the end, but should it be considered a Christmas movie? You may not agree with those die-hard *Die Hard* fans, but in 2016 DISH Network reported that 1.3 million people watched *Die Hard* during the holiday season, bringing in more viewers than *Miracle on 34th Street* or *The Santa Clause*. Can 1.3 million people be wrong? Of course they can, but what does it mean that so many seem to enjoy *Die Hard* during the holiday season?

Sometimes things don't appear to have anything to do with Christmas at all, but the Christmas story is definitely at their heart.

Wherever you side on the *Die Hard* Christmas movie controversy, it highlights the fact that the Christmas message doesn't always accompany Christmas music and decorations. Even when something looks like Christmas, we have to judge whether the Christmas story really is present. It happens the opposite way, too. Sometimes things don't appear to have anything to do with Christmas at all, but the Christmas story is definitely at their heart.

The Christmas message isn't always obvious. As a vocal performance major I remember rehearsing "This Is My Box," a tenor aria from Gian Carlo Menotti's *Amahl and the Night Visitors*. Even though I was not successful in mastering the difficult song, the long hours in the practice room gave me a great appreciation for this curious opera. *Amahl and the Night Visitors* is a one-act opera, the first opera to be specifically composed for television in

1951. Menotti was inspired to compose this "for children" opera because, "In Italy we have no Santa Claus. I suppose that Santa Claus is much too busy with American children to be able to handle Italian children as well. Our gifts were brought to us by the Three Kings, instead."[2] *Amahl and the Night Visitors* is the story of a shepherd boy hindered with a crutch and his mother wrestling with poverty. One night three visitors come to seek lodging on their way to pay homage to a very special child who had been born. While Amahl's mother is making preparations to host the three visitors, Amahl badgers the visitors with questions, revealing to the audience that the three guests are the three wise men from Matthew's Gospel.

After Amahl and his mother gather the neighbors together to help feed and entertain the guests, the three kings settle down for the evening. While they sleep, Amahl's mother attempts to steal gold from King Melchior. When she is discovered, Amahl desperately tries to come to her defense. When the king considers their desperate situation and Amahl's great love for his mother, King Melchior gives the gold to them, saying that the child they seek will not need it. His kingdom will not be built on wealth. Overwhelmed with guilt, Amahl's mother wants to offer a gift, but has nothing to spare. So Amahl offers his crutch in return for the king's gold. After handing away his crutch, he discovers that he's been healed and can walk freely. The curtain closes as the kings ask to take Amahl with them, so he can personally offer his crutch to this miraculous child in gratitude for his healing.

Amahl and the Night Visitors is not an opera that you will hear on the radio after Thanksgiving. Rarely will you find it performed in local churches in lieu of the annual children's Christmas pageant. The music doesn't contain any of the familiar jingle bells or reindeer-centered imagery we usually associate with the holiday season. It poignantly wrestles with images of poverty and desperation which rarely fit our sanctuary Christmas décor. The opera feels weird and almost foreign, which may be the point. The message of a child bringing healing to the lame and an end to desperation for the poor is certainly part of the Christmas story, but the packaging is unfamiliar. In other words, it doesn't look like Christmas, but it most certainly is.

The story of the Wise Men in Matthew's Gospel is peculiar, and the meaning behind men from the East offering the Christ Child gold, frankincense, and myrrh doesn't seem to feel as "Christmasy" as angels, shepherds, and "Silent Night." This story about those from the east following the light of the glory of God, bowing at his feet, offering him gifts, is the fulfillment of Isaiah 60.

> *Nations shall come to your light,*
> *and kings to the brightness of your dawn.*
>
> *Lift up your eyes and look around;*
> *they all gather together, they come to you;*
> *your sons shall come from far away,*
> *and your daughters shall be carried on their*
> *nurses' arms.*
> *Then you shall see and be radiant;*
> *your heart shall thrill and rejoice,*
> *because the abundance of the sea shall be brought to you,*
> *the wealth of the nations shall come to you.*

A multitude of camels shall cover you,
    the young camels of Midian and Ephah;
    all those from Sheba shall come.
They shall bring gold and frankincense,
    and shall proclaim the praise of the Lord.
                    (Isaiah 60:3-6 NRSV)

The wise men offer gold for Christ's kingship. They offer incense as a sign of devotion or prayer. They also offer myrrh as a sign that his kingship is rooted in his redeeming death. These travelers from the east seem to really know God's story, even better than King Herod who seemed rather confused that they showed up to the palace bearing gifts. But this story is so much more than our typical "Christmasy" reading of the importance of giving gifts. This story is about the forgiveness of Babylon, that great enemy of Israel. The wise men bowing to Christ is a beautiful and biblical way to reveal that in Christ, even Babylon can be forgiven. The forgiveness of Babylon doesn't feel like Christmas, but it most certainly is.

A few years ago I noticed the Nativity of a local church in Shreveport looked different from what I had remembered. Instead of the pleasant and peaceful holy family gathered together in a well-lit manger, Mary, Joseph, and the baby Jesus were all in separate cages, calling to mind that families seeking asylum were being separated at the United States's southern border. It was a shocking image, and it's supposed to be. Thinking about the Holy Family seeking asylum in Egypt to escape a bloodthirsty King Herod (Matthew 2:13-23) doesn't seem to fit the beauty and grandeur of our Christmas cantatas, but it is a crucial element of Jesus's infancy narrative. Jesus's flight into Egypt is a reminder that "Thus says the LORD of hosts: Render true judgments, show kindness and mercy to one another; do not oppress the widow, the orphan, the alien, or the poor; and do not devise evil in your hearts against one another" (Zechariah 7:9-10). There are multiple verses in the Hebrew Scriptures and the New Testament about showing hospitality and offering justice for the foreigner or "alien" among us.

The flight into Egypt isn't only a story about justice for those seeking asylum. Much like the story of the wise men is about the forgiveness of Babylon, the story of the Holy Family fleeing to Egypt is about Egypt's redemption. Since the Book of Exodus Egypt has been a symbol of slavery and bondage. In Matthew's Gospel Egypt is transformed into an image of safe haven and peace. In other words, the Christ Child is the one who forgives Babylon and redeems Egypt. There is so much more to this Christmas story that we so often miss. Babylon's forgiveness and Egypt's redemption don't feel like Christmas, but they most certainly are.

Could it be that the Grinch might know more about the Christmas story than the Whos?

Could it be that the Grinch might know more about the Christmas story than the Whos? Could it be that his frustration is that he thinks the Whos have been missing the point of the

YOU'RE A MEAN ONE

The most famous song from the Grinch 1966 television special is "You're a Mean One, Mr. Grinch" sung by Thurl Ravenscroft. The song became a laundry list of gross adjectives describing the Grinch as a bad banana peel, dead tomato, and a sauerkraut and toadstool sandwich. Geisel really felt that this appropriately made the Grinch even more slimy and detestable than did his original work. The music also slinks about, and often uses a downward scale in the bass line, communicating the stereotypical and fanciful villainous theme needed to introduce a character such as the Grinch.

season all along? He lives alone on Mt. Crumpit and never seems to be invited to the party. Their perceived lack of hospitality certainly doesn't fit our Christmas story. I don't think that's why the Grinch is upset. I think it's more likely that he's bothered by their noise and toys. Anything deeper than that certainly isn't explicit in Seuss's book, but maybe this is part of what the story wants us to feel. The Grinch is other. He is an outsider. With all of the merriment and singing, his loneliness must sting. It's like seeing the Nativity in cages. We might not be able to articulate why it's so shocking, but the shock wakes us up into diving deeper into the Christmas story.

The Grinch's loneliness and animosity toward Christmas don't feel like a part of the Christmas story. They feel like an intrusion, something that has to do with the Whos' celebration only because it opposes and defines itself against their merrymaking. But as we saw in the first chapter, hatred and suffering and other painful realities are a part of our world, and Jesus's arrival into this world, pain and all, is at the heart of the Christmas story.

Does Die Hard *count as a Christmas movie? Why or why not? What makes a Christmas movie a Christmas movie?*

Have you ever seen a Nativity scene or other depiction of Jesus's birth that felt jarring? What made it so?

The story of the magi hints at the redemption of Babylon and Egypt. What does the inclusion of these historic enemies of God's people in the Messiah's birth communicate about the salvation he brings?

He Chose...Wisely

Near the end of *Indiana Jones and the Last Crusade,* Indiana has to choose the correct cup of Christ among seemingly hundreds in order to save his father's life. If he chooses the wrong chalice, life will be taken from him. If he chooses wisely, life will be offered. He spends just a moment or two gazing at the jewel-encrusted, golden cups, and finally chooses a simple wooden cup saying, "This is the cup of a carpenter." He dips the vessel into a spring of water, takes a sip, and he hears the ancient Templar Knight take his time saying, "You have chosen...wisely." Is it wrong for the cup on the altar or table to be made with fine metal representing the preciousness of Christ's blood? Probably not, but there is great truth in this classic scene. Choosing the cup of a carpenter, remembering that Jesus was born into poverty, proclaiming that Jesus's birth announcement was offered to shepherds will always be a wise choice. There were no guarantees that Indiana was correct, but he knew the story well.

The interesting thing about this scene is that I'm not convinced that choosing the right cup was really the point. I think Indiana would have succeeded regardless of which chalice he used. What he "chose wisely" was his intention for the cup. He didn't want the cup of Christ for himself or world domination; rather he wanted to save his father's life. Some things look like Christmas, but really don't have anything to do with Christ's birth. Other things don't look like Christmas, but seem to have the Christmas story at their heart. Regardless of whether something "feels" like Christmas or not, the point is for our celebrations to authentically share the mystery and miracle of the Incarnation while also maintaining a life-giving presence in the life of the church.

My wife, Christie, has a favorite Nativity set. Many years ago her paternal grandfather carved a Nativity scene out of wood. The pieces were simple silhouette blocks that almost fit together like a children's big block puzzle. This Nativity set was then given to her maternal grandfather who further carved the pieces, adding specific details and making them less abstract. The Nativity set is beautifully simple and homemade, at once both universal and unique. With each generation the Nativity set slightly changes. It still represents the story of Christ's birth, but also takes on the characteristics of its current host. Our Christmas traditions on the whole are like this Nativity set. The original story was simple and beautiful, and over many generations and celebrations, the story changes to fit our cultural context. If we do it well, we retain the heart of the story even as we celebrate in new ways to speak in our world. Yet if we aren't careful we may unintentionally transform a simple Nativity set to be only a reflection of our story, with little witness to the meaning and significance of the Incarnation.

In the Jim Carrey movie version of the Grinch, Cindy Lou Who recognizes that the Whos' Christmas celebrations have become more about the Whos than the holiday. She also sympathizes with the Grinch and wants to include him in their festivities. The Grinch's inclusion is rejected by the Whos at first, but imagine if it wasn't. Imagine that Cindy Lou succeeds right away in her attempt to change the Whos' celebration. We would probably have a much shorter and less dramatic story. But, of course, the Whos do resist this change, which seems natural to us. We don't have to stretch our imaginations too far to recognize that changing our Christmas traditions meets with resistance. Every year I joke with the congregation, wondering how Jesus could possibly have been born before "Silent Night" was written. It almost seems inconceivable to have Christmas Eve without singing "Silent Night" by candlelight. If anyone suggested replacing that song with another, it would certainly face opposition.

The year 2020 was a difficult one, with a great deal of improvisation and on-the-fly changes. For good or ill, Advent and Christmas looked very different that year. As difficult as the last year has been, it offered the opportunity to reevaluate our traditional celebrations and ask what it means to glorify God in new and different ways, retaining the heart of the story. It would have been difficult, maybe even impossible, to make those kinds of changes without a crisis to make them necessary. It will be difficult to retain them, or at least the best of them, instead of just defaulting back to the way we always did it before. Sometimes it takes a crisis to spur needed change, something to shock us out of the ordinary.

One year when I was an associate pastor, we did a dramatic reading of John the Baptist preaching to the crowd on the second Sunday of Advent. Being the associate, I was tasked with portraying this firebrand of a prophet. I entered from the back of the sanctuary without warning and started shouting:

*"You brood of vipers! Who warned you to flee from
the wrath to come? Bear fruit worthy of repentance.
Do not presume to say to yourselves, 'We have
Abraham as our ancestor'; for I tell you, God is able
from these stones to raise up children to Abraham.
Even now the ax is lying at the root of the trees; every
tree therefore that does not bear good fruit is cut
down and thrown into the fire. I baptize you with
water for repentance, but one who is more powerful
than I is coming after me; I am not worthy to carry
his sandals. He will baptize you with the Holy Spirit
and fire. His winnowing fork is in his hand, and
he will clear his threshing floor and will gather his
wheat into the granary; but the chaff he will burn
with unquenchable fire."*

(Matthew 3:7b-12 NRSV)

My dramatic rendition must have made quite an impression. One member, who I recall was emphatically nodding in agreement with my angry yelling, found me after the service wanting me to gather folks from his Sunday school class for a pet project of his. The program he had in mind had much more to do with his personal politics than it did with anything resembling the ministry of our local church. He told me that John the Baptist's words were the kind of fire we needed to get his political rallies off the ground.

He loved the idea of having an opportunity to call others "You brood of vipers," but of course he missed the point of John's message. Although John seems angrier than we might expect,

John's ministry and message always point to Jesus. John prepares the way, not to himself, but to the coming Messiah. We too often tragically see ourselves as John in the story, and not as the brood of vipers pridefully proclaiming our own importance as Abraham's heir. Over time, as our Christmas celebrations lean into our own preferences and traditions, we just might need an "ax at the root of the tree" in order to bring us back to pointing toward Christ instead of ourselves.

I'm not saying that the Grinch is John the Baptist, but the similarity is striking. Both are loners, seemingly aggravated and unhappy with the celebrations that they see around them. Both want to do away with what they understand to be an obnoxious and self-centered observance. Although the Grinch isn't pointing to Jesus, his "winnowing fork" does become the catalyst for a transformed heart. Maybe having a touch of the Grinch isn't an altogether bad thing. Maybe we should refuse to replant some of the things that were uprooted over the last year. Maybe without the distraction of the bejeweled golden chalice that we have built, we might "choose wisely" in order to create an environment that, whether you're singing "Jingle Bells" or watching *Die Hard*, points to the life-giving mystery of God-in-the-flesh.

How do we celebrate the birth of Christ in our own way, while retaining the heart of the story? How do we know when we've gone too far and made the celebration more about us than about Christ?

What similarities do you see between the Grinch and John the Baptist?

Where might you need a jarring, harsh message to spark a fresh look at the ways you practice your faith, especially in this season of Advent?

WHEN THERE IS NO HOPE

I love the outdoors. What I love about the outdoors is that it's outdoors, and not inside my home. Humanity has spent thousands of years perfecting the barrier that separates the outdoors from indoors. Generally speaking, humanity appreciates this kind of order. Outdoors are out and indoors are in. You cannot vote at seventeen years old, but you can vote when you are eighteen. If you are from Alabama, you can be either a fan of Alabama or Auburn. Order makes things simple and expected, defined and clear. These are not bad things. What we soon discover, though, is that Advent is not simple or expected; it's neither defined nor clear.

At the beginning of Advent, many of us do something rather peculiar. We go and find a tree that is growing in the outdoors, and we chop it down and bring it indoors. In a small way, we blur the lines of order. Of course, order eventually wins because the tree begins to die, and it must be moved back into the outdoors. But for a moment the lines we have drawn are transgressed; the order we have set up becomes confused.

The season of Advent to the rest of the Christian year is like poetry against a blueprint. A blueprint is exact and precise. It has to be. Here are where the walls of the house are supposed to be. Poetry bends the rules; it leaves room for interpretation and the unexpected. Poetry is a terrible way to build a house, but it is a way to make a house a home. Advent is like poetry in the sense that we hope for something that has already happened, and that equation makes no sense on a blueprint. Specifically, an Advent hope is an exercise in poetry because against what the data is reporting, against what your eyes see and your ears hear, hope offers a different narrative.

Poetry is a terrible way to build a house, but it is a way to make a house a home.

This is why Isaiah is so important. During Isaiah's ministry, Israel in the north and Judah in the south were two separate kingdoms, and sometimes they were at war with each other. Assyria, the capital of which is Nineveh, that great and terrible city you may remember from the Book of Jonah, has already destroyed Israel, and their eyes are set on Judah and Jerusalem. Even though Judah has seen the destruction the Assyrians have wrought upon Israel, even though Jerusalem's destruction seems to be inevitable, even though, as Scripture says, the trees have been left as stumps, Isaiah offers poetry. He offers hope. "A shoot will grow up from the stump of Jesse; a branch will sprout from his roots" (Isaiah 11:1). It is not just any shoot. It is not just any leader. This new shoot, or Nazareth, will have the spirit of the Lord resting upon him. This shoot will know wisdom, not just information. He will have understanding, not just data. He will judge not by what the eye sees and what the ears hear. He will not just offer the word of God but will be the poetry of God, because the ordered lines between humanity and the divine will be blurred in his own person, so that where one ends and the other begins will be indistinguishable.

When the tree is placed in our living rooms, it signals that the lines we have drawn in the world have now become blurred and we are ready for hope. As I mentioned in the previous chapter, we begin Advent with peace because we must be at peace with our self, our neighbor, and our God before we begin to have the holy imagination for hope. In other words, peace offers the order necessary for hope to begin bending the rules.

In the first year of seminary you learn Old Testament, New Testament, theology, and church history. By the end of your first year, you metaphorically build this God box. After you survey Scripture and learn orthodox doctrine and how the church grew, how the creeds came to be, and how the church grew and split, and who the true believers were and who the heretics were, God fits quite nicely in your box. You leave that first year thinking, "This is who the triune God is—Father, Son, and Spirit, and this is what it means to be the church." You're thinking, "All I need is a microphone and a Bible and I'm ready to start a church." You have drafted the blueprint...and then you go back for your second year, and your professors take a sledgehammer to your box and bust it wide open. Then you build your box again, and then they bust that one open too, and so on and so forth until you finally realize that God doesn't fit in a box at all.

Think about math. In first grade you are told in subtraction the top number needs to be bigger than the bottom number.

You have built a box into which you can understand subtraction. Then a few grades higher the teacher begins to write the smaller number on the top, and at first you think you can't do that, or the teacher has made a mistake. But the teacher hasn't...you're just about to learn negative numbers. Instead of one number on the top of another, you now are taught about a number line that goes on to infinity in both directions. Then you learn about irrational numbers. Then you move on to imaginary numbers, and then eventually your equations have no numbers at all. Each new lesson is a foundation on which the next one will be built.

In the same way, being at peace gives you the foundation necessary so that when your box is eventually broken down, you know for what to hope and that you don't give up. Being at peace helps us discern the difference between a hope that poetically defies the rules and a chaos that only is destructive. I talk about bringing a tree into your living room, but what if you don't have a living room? Many churches, ours included, collect clothing for community members in need. One reason we do that is as a reminder that we must be at peace with our neighbors, and part of that peace is keeping chaos at bay, the chaos of not knowing when your next meal will be, not knowing if you will be safe during the cold weather. May the tree that we bring in from the outside be a hopeful reminder that there are some things that are outside that should be in and not simply returned to the outside when the season is over. Let us seek peace so that we know for what to hope.

> *The wolf shall live with the lamb,*
> *the leopard shall lie down with the kid,*
> *the calf and the lion and the fatling together,*

and a little child shall lead them.
The cow and the bear shall graze,
their young shall lie down together;
and the lion shall eat straw like the ox.
The nursing child shall play over the hole of the asp,
and the weaned child shall put its hand on the
adder's den.
They will not hurt or destroy
on all my holy mountain;
for the earth will be full of the knowledge of the Lord
as the waters cover the sea.

(Isaiah 11:6-9 NRSV)

Peace brings us into hope, and that hope shows us an everlasting peace.

Peace brings us into hope, and that hope shows us an everlasting peace. You no longer need a God box holding in your perception of God against someone else's because the earth will be full of the knowledge of the Lord as the waters cover the sea. The Christmas tree is a tree of hope because as long as it is nurtured, it is evergreen. It carries upon itself the symbols of our faith. It shows us for what to hope. This is the beautiful thing about the Angel Tree many churches have in their narthex. As the ornaments disappear, so does a need. The more bare the tree becomes, the more fulfilled the surrounding community is. Eventually the tree will be completely bare, its branches removed, a cross bar affixed upon it, and upon the tree Jesus will die and then be resurrected.

Hope is poetry, not chaos. It's not the Grinch stealing away the Whos' things in the night; it's the Whos waking up the next morning and singing just the same. Hope is the kind of language that inspires and builds and ignites change to the point when change is no longer needed. Hope is a destination when you finally discover that you don't need to build a God box anymore because you have finally realized that God is bigger.

A tree from the outside is indeed a beautiful and hopeful picture. What's even more beautiful is a tree that has no ornaments because our story has already been told and the needs of God's people are being met. And what's even more beautiful is not chopping down the tree at all and letting it flourish and grow right where it is, because the poetry of Advent hasn't brought the outside in, but the inside out to where the church itself no longer has walls because we have finally realized after building and destroying our God box over and over again, that God doesn't fit in a box. After all, our ultimate hope is that heaven and earth will be one. God will be with God's people—Emmanuel.

In what ways does Advent blur the lines we usually rely on to bring order to our faith and to our world?

When has the Holy Spirit disrupted your previous understanding of God? What did you learn, and how did your faith grow as a result?

When has your own sense of control and peace been challenged by Jesus?

CHAPTER THREE

WHEN LIGHT SHINES

When our children were little, our families lived between four to six hours away. For my wife, Christie, and me, Thanksgiving was less a day set apart to give thanks for God's blessings and more a weeklong tour of South Louisiana to visit family. Our first stop was Baton Rouge, and we knew that we were spending the night, so the first thing we did was to set up the children's rooms for the evening. One year, as we were setting the beds and plugging in the sleepy-time lullaby radio, we noticed that there was no night light in the room. If there's no night light in the room, you might as well give the kids chocolate cake before bed because they're not going to sleep. So, we feverishly searched the house for a night light, and we thankfully found one just in time for bed. Light is important, often taken for granted, and children remind us of its beauty and security. When the bedroom is dark, just a glimmer of light will do to keep the monsters in the closet at bay.

In the middle of the night the Grinch is up to no good. He enters one of the Who's homes to steal away anything and everything that might have something to do with Christmas. The job seems easy enough. The stockings, the presents, and even the food is stowed away in the Grinch's sacks, and sent up the chimney with ease. There's no hesitation or remorse. He doesn't stop to second-guess or reconsider. Like a champion bagger at the checkout line during a holiday rush, the Grinch bags everything together, only momentarily leaving the tree behind, and he does it all in the darkness of night.

Darkness is an interesting thing. The absence of light can help hide things we don't want people to see and obscure the things to which we'd rather not call attention, but darkness isn't altogether bad. Our other senses are heightened when our eyes have to take a less dominant role. I love putting lots of candles on the table in the sanctuary, and I'd be lying if I said I always remembered to extinguish them at the conclusion of each service. It's hard to notice a single candle burning next to our copper-covered cross when the sanctuary lights are full. Sometimes I've come back to the church on Sunday evenings when everything is dark and quiet, and it doesn't take long for me to have a moment of panic when I notice a candle left lit in the sanctuary. After saying a quick prayer of thanksgiving that nothing caught fire, and that our head of trustees didn't see it, I quickly blow the candle out and continue my meditation.

The only reason I notice the candle at times like this is because everything else is quiet, still, and dark. Maybe this is why Luke records that Jesus was born in the evening. "Nearby shepherds were living in the fields, guarding their sheep at night. The Lord's angel stood before them, the Lord's glory shone around them, and they were terrified" (Luke 2:8-9). There's nothing in Scripture that says Jesus had to have been born at night. It's not the fulfillment of any prophecy or demand from God. But maybe the glory of the Lord accompanying the angel seemed just a bit brighter and even more noticeable in the dark. Maybe this is what John means when he wrote, "The light shines in the darkness, / and the darkness doesn't extinguish the light" (John 1:5). It's not that darkness is necessary to see light, but darkness certainly makes light more noticeable.

When the Grinch begins shoving the Who family's Christmas tree into the chimney at night, he notices young Cindy Lou Who standing and watching him. She asks why the Grinch is taking the tree away. Without so much as a blink, the Grinch says that the lights on one side of the tree aren't working, and he's taking the tree to his workshop where he will fix it up and bring it back. I don't think it's an accident that the Grinch calls attention to lights not working. He lies so quickly to the young child, and when a lie is effortless, there's always a truth just under the surface. A Christmas tree with broken lights is like a Grinch with a heart two sizes too small. The tree can still hold ornaments and be a placeholder for gifts, but without the lights, there's something missing. The Grinch still has a heart. It's just not big enough to be much good. There's something missing. The Grinch doesn't try to quickly scurry away, or yell angrily back at Cindy. He conceals the truth, and the only reason one tries to hide the truth is because you know the truth is powerful.

The Grinch still has a heart. It's just not big enough to be much good. There's something missing.

We hear from Scripture that the "truth will set you free" (John 8:32), but that doesn't mean the truth is easy to hear. Deep down I think the Grinch knows what he's doing is wrong. It reminds me of when my oldest daughter was young. One afternoon I walked into her room, and anything that had been on a shelf was now on the floor. Her room was a complete disaster. I asked her what happened and why her room was so messy. Knowing that Daddy likes rooms to be tidy, she looked up at me without hesitation and said, "I was just looking for something beautiful." I replied, "Well, why don't you look for something beautiful while putting everything back where it belongs."

Light can provide comfort, security, and hope, but it can also bring about death and destruction. The prophet Jeremiah wrote both challenging and hopeful words with the aid of glimmering light, but this was not peaceful candlelight that lit his room. He was writing amidst the destruction of the Temple in Jerusalem. The light flickering in the distance was that of a fire as the Temple smoldered in ruin. The light he saw was the light of hopelessness. The Temple was gone, which meant that God and God's promises had departed. In the midst of ashes, his words communicate a resounding "No!" to the darkness surrounding him and his people. He writes, "The time is coming, declares the LORD, when I will fulfill my gracious promise with the people of Israel and Judah" (Jeremiah 33:14).

This is a stinging "No!" to the world. Israel had been destroyed by the Assyrians years before, never to return. Judah saw this happen, and now it was happening to them by the Babylonians. They knew that destruction led to an end of the people and an end to their story with God. And now they are in despair because it's happening to them. "The time is coming, declares the LORD, when I will fulfill my gracious promise with the people of Israel and Judah. In those days and at that time I will raise up a righteous branch from David's line, who will do what is just and right in the land" (Jeremiah 33:14-15).

Not long after Hurricane Katrina devastated New Orleans, my mother called me, and rather spur of the moment, asked Christie and me to join her and my father on a trip to Walt Disney World. I said, "OK, if I have to." While we were there, I asked my mother why she wanted to take the trip, why the sense of urgency? She said, "I needed to see something alive." When I finally made it to New Orleans after our trip, I knew what she was talking about. Everything was dead. Trees had fallen, grass was drowned, buildings were empty. I'm sure the scene was similar to what Noah saw when getting off the ark. The renderings we typically see when Noah is getting off the ark are of a green and lush utopia with birds flying and lions grinning, but we tend to forget that anything and everything that wasn't on the ark had died. It must have looked like the Ninth Ward in New Orleans.

What amazing faith Noah had to get off the boat and begin rebuilding the world. An olive branch in a dove's mouth confirmed for Noah that dry land had begun to appear and that it would soon be safe to depart the ark. And when Noah and the animals got off the boat, God made a covenant with Noah and gave him a sign, a visible symbol of his faith. The sign was a rainbow, an effect of light in the sky. A branch and light were signs for Noah bringing hope for the future. In the same way, light in the sky signified the birth of Jesus, the righteous branch springing up from David. See, in the church we don't count down to Christmas. We count forward to a new hope, and new life given to us by the Messiah, the baby to be born on the outskirts of town. That's why the branch is such a beautiful symbol. It's not a stopwatch counting down. It is life itself growing and moving forward into fruition, the hope of God's promise being fulfilled.

On our way back from the great South Louisiana tour one year, we entered our neighborhood with the children cheering from the backseat. The houses on either side of our street were lit from top to bottom with Christmas lights. The lights were beautiful, and certainly a welcomed sight, but these lights are not just for decoration. Adults don't like the dark either. When it begins getting dark around 4:30 in the afternoon, we cover our homes in light. Christmas lights are one of the first glimpses of the changing season. When darkness creeps into our lives, we say, "No!" by turning on the lights. The same holds true in the church.

I suppose we could call attention to peace, hope, love, and joy by using berries on an Advent wreath, or a North Pole thermometer, but we choose to light candles. We have chosen light to be the way in which we celebrate the coming of Christ.

Recall a time when darkness, either literally or figuratively, helped you see or notice something more clearly than you would have otherwise.

When have you experienced light in the midst of darkness?

Think about how central light is to our celebration of Advent and Christmas. Why do you think this is the case?

TELLING THE TRUTH

Do you know the legend of the Belsnickel? According to German legend, the Belsnickel was a mysterious creature who would check in on children a couple of weeks before Christmas to see if they were behaving. He would rap on the window, throw candy on the floor, and if you jumped too soon to receive the candy, he would rap you with his walking stick. My grandmother would tell us a similar story, though in her version the Belsnickel would visit in the weeks after Christmas to make sure that you were still minding your manners after receiving your presents. If you were misbehaving, the Belsnickel would come in the middle of the night, steal away your toys, and there was nothing you could do to get them back. It's a rather frightening tale when you're a child, but the message was clear: You cannot fool Santa. You may have been well behaved in order to get presents, but you must maintain your manners for the long winter break, or he will send his Belsnickel to take the toys back. As a parent, I fully understand why this story exists, and I'm not ashamed to tell you that my children know this folktale quite well.

The interaction between the Grinch and Cindy Lou Who is like an ironic Belsnickel tale. The Grinch is stealing away all of the children's toys, but his theft is for his own sordid enjoyment. Cindy is like the mysterious Belsnickel figure urging the expression of a moral compass, but instead of rapping the Grinch with a walking stick, she asks a simple question: "Why are you taking our Christmas tree?" It's a fair question. Cindy Lou Who is like this tiny spark of light twinkling in a rather dark portion of the story. Children tend to ask the kind of questions we grown-ups neglect or have forgotten how to ask, like, "If God is big enough to create the mountains, how can God also live in our heart?" As we age, sometimes it's as if our vision becomes increasingly narrow. We often grow into a particular worldview and live by assumptions according to the way we think things should be. In a way, we develop blind spots as if our peripheral vision disappeared with our childhood.

It takes a moment of humility to recognize that we have blind spots. It's a part of our human condition. It's not a sin to have blind spots, but not correcting for them just might be. The reason we have mirrors on our car is because we don't have eyes in the back of head. If we didn't have corrective mirrors, we and those around us might get hurt. The same holds true for the cultural blind spots we carry with us, the assumptions we hold in our day-to-day lives. Without growing in faith and correcting for our falsely held assumptions, we cannot live into our fullest selves.

**Without growing in faith and correcting…
we cannot live into our fullest selves.**

Jesus had blind spots. It may sound strange to consider that Jesus didn't see everything, but like us, Jesus also didn't have eyes in the back of his head. The Christian faith teaches that Jesus was fully human and fully divine—not sometimes human and sometimes divine, but indivisibly human and divine. This is a difficult teaching to wrestle with. In a worship setting we have a very easy time talking about Jesus's divinity, but if we aren't careful we begin to lean away from Christian teaching and lean into a heresy called "Docetism." Docetism refers to a belief and teaching by some in the early church, refuted as a heresy in the early fourth century, that Jesus only *appeared* to be human. He only *appeared* to hunger and thirst, only *appeared* to get frustrated, only *appeared* to suffer and rise from the dead. If this were the case, the early church concluded, then Jesus only *appeared* to save us. The truth is that Jesus was fully human.

The Christmas mystery is that Jesus was both fully divine and fully human, but how human is that exactly? The letter to the Hebrews says, "because we don't have a high priest who

GOING ALL OUT

The production team spared no expense with producing the Grinch television special. An average episode of the popular *The Flintstones* primetime cartoon used roughly 2,000 individual drawings for 30 minutes of screen time; the Grinch special used over 25,000 drawings. Maurice Noble, who was rather starstruck when meeting Geisel, was hired to complete the picturesque backgrounds for the special. Geisel constantly told Noble to make the backgrounds enriching and schmaltzy, to which Noble replied, "You don't argue too long with God."[1] Eventually Noble created 250 backgrounds for the special, which is more than twice the amount for a regular thirty-minute program.

can't sympathize with our weaknesses but instead one who was tempted in every way that we are, except without sin" (Hebrews 4:15). How does all of this work? Let's think about our blind spots for a moment. If you are celebrating Christmas in Hawaii this year, you may think twice about getting into the water out of fear of a shark attack, but you probably don't worry about walking near palm trees. But statistically speaking, falling coconuts are much more likely and much more deadly. As a different example, maybe you're hanging garland on the chancel rail, but you forgot your ruler and you don't know how much you'll need. You know that your backyard fence is about thirty feet, and you can make a quick eyeball judgment by comparing what you know about your fence to what you don't know about the chancel. Let's say you're checking the weather forecast from your favorite news source and they predict that you'll be having a snowy Christmas Eve, so you make sure to put a coat in the trunk of your car before you head out to worship.

All of these are examples different biases or lenses through which we interpret the world. We make mental shortcuts, assumptions, based on what we already know. We assume that sharks pose a threat because we saw *Jaws*, and there isn't a movie series to put a fear of coconuts in our heart. We assume that length measurements will be roughly the same at our house and in our sanctuary. There is nothing wrong with making assumptions like these; it is part of what it means to be human. These examples might sound simple and silly, but they illustrate just how many assumptions we make on a daily basis. If we are unable to recognize the extent of them, we might find ourselves believing our assumptions to be unwavering truth. Let's say that it doesn't snow on Christmas Eve as your favorite weather forecaster had predicted. It might be easy enough to simply accept that the forecast wasn't quite right, but there is sometimes a great temptation to squint and peer out into the darkness and think we see a few flurries because we cannot accept that the information we received wasn't quite right.

Lots of lenses affect the way we understand the world. Our emotions sometimes cloud our decisions, or our love of the status quo makes us hesitant to take calculated risks, especially since we tend to feel loss as being more powerful than gains received. I often have to remind myself that the 4 percent of negative emails don't outweigh the 96 percent of positive feedback, but that's easier said than done.

The point is, we have blind spots. We don't see everything as clearly as maybe we should. Here's the wrestling: Jesus had blind spots too, because blind spots are fully human things. For example, the parable of the good Samaritan makes little sense if Jesus wasn't fully aware of the ethnic hatred between Jews and Samaritans. How does Jesus explain how the prodigal son hit rock bottom? Well, he said that he was a pig farmer, and as a Jewish person, being a pig farmer is probably the worst profession there is. Jesus got angry, making a whip and driving out the money changers from the Temple. Jesus became frustrated, telling the disciples, "How long will I put up with you?" (Matthew 17:17). Jesus didn't know everything. The Gospel of Luke says that after Jesus was in the Temple as a twelve-year-old, Jesus grew in wisdom and favor, and the only way you can grow in wisdom is if you don't know everything at the outset. When is the end, Jesus? He answered the disciples saying, "I don't know. Only the Father knows" (see Mark 13:32). Jesus was emotional, weeping over Lazarus's death and lamenting over Jerusalem. Jesus faced all of the same challenges and limitations that characterize human life, including incomplete knowledge about his world.

We have blind spots. We don't see everything as clearly as maybe we should.... it is not a sin to have blind spots, but not correcting for them just may be.

Again, it is not a sin to have blind spots, but not correcting for them just may be. The humble message of Christmas is that God put on flesh and entered into our humanity—blind spots and all. This is why Cindy Lou Who's question is so important. "Why are you taking our Christmas tree?" If the Grinch had taken a moment to consider Cindy's question, he may have realized one of his own blind spots. He may have understood that he wasn't seeing everything he needed to see. Unfortunately, his vision was too narrow. In a manner of speaking, the lights on the tree indeed were out.

Do you have any Christmas traditions that others might find peculiar or unfamiliar, as some may find the legend of Belsnickel?

Why do children tend to ask big, fundamental questions more readily than adults? What can adults learn from this?

How do you respond to the idea of Jesus having blind spots? Do you find it hopeful or challenging that he had to learn and grow in the same way we all do?

EVEN THE CRUMBS WERE TOO SMALL

The Grinch sends Cindy Lou Who back to bed with a glass of water and then begins to empty out their home of anything and everything that has something to do with Christmas. It's not enough that he stole away any hint of Christmas; the Grinch leaves only crumbs behind, morsels too small even for a mouse. House after house, the Grinch sneaks down the chimney, and takes almost everything. The Grinch may despise the Whos' excessive celebration, but the Grinch seems to have a compulsion all his own. Why does he leave nothing behind? Wouldn't just taking the presents make his point loud and clear? It'd be one thing if the Grinch were stealing the gifts so that he might horde them for himself; that sermon is easy to write. Instead, he plans to dump everything off the side of a cliff. It's like that great scene in *The Dark Knight* where the Joker burns a huge mountain of money. When asked why he's doing it he replies, "It's not about the money. It's about sending a message." What message was the Grinch trying to communicate?

One of the gifts the wise men bring to the Christ Child is gold, symbolizing Jesus's kingship (Matthew 2:11). Have you ever considered what Jesus, Mary, and Joseph did with this precious gift? There are several traditions, including one in which the gifts were used to pay for Jesus's education and another in which the gold financed the Holy Family's escape into Egypt. The real answer is that Scripture doesn't tell us, but Scripture does tell us that Jesus had a very particular view of how we should treat the treasure in our possession: "Stop collecting treasures for your own benefit on earth, where moth and rust eat them and where thieves break in and steal them. Instead collect treasures for yourselves in heaven, where moth and rust don't eat them and where thieves don't break in and steal them. Where your treasure is, there your heart will be also" (Matthew 6:19-21).

Not to store up treasure for yourself is easier said than done. One year when my family was moving to a new church, we called a local moving company to come to the house to assess how big a moving truck we would need. Unsurprisingly, the representative made a reservation for the largest truck in their fleet. It's not that our items were precious, valuable, or expensive, but we had lots of furniture handed down to us from friends and family, and with young children we had high chairs, walkers, mini trampolines, dollhouses... you name it.

The truck arrived and the movers started loading all our belongings. When the truck was about halfway full, and it appeared that they had barely made a dent with all our boxes, I asked the driver when the next truck was coming. His confused look made my stomach turn. "There is no other truck," he replied, looking at me as if I had been dressed as a circus clown. "What happens if this doesn't all fit on the truck?" I asked, while wondering why I would even have to ask such a question. "I don't know. Probably rent a U-Haul or something. Do you have a buddy with a truck?"

Do I have a buddy with a truck?! That's your answer?! First of all, I do have friends with trucks, but we were moving five hours away. There's not enough pizza and beverages on the planet to convince someone to take a quick ten-hour round trip to help cover a bad professional moving company estimate. Secondly, we were living in a parsonage, which means that the next pastor's family was on the way later that day to move in. We started calling everyone we knew who wouldn't be offended with such a crazy ask. Thankfully one of my friends found an available rentable trailer about an hour or so away that would get us closer to containing all of our things, but my Toyota Camry is ill-equipped for hauling. Another friend just happened to have been traveling from New Orleans to Shreveport later that afternoon and was willing to help us out. At the end of the day we called in every favor we had available and managed to successfully move everything to our new home.

Store up treasures in heaven is easy to say, but when you are potentially leaving a quarter of your belongings behind, it's more difficult to believe. We almost seem hardwired to collect things, whether they be souvenirs marking fond memories, or items in the workshops you just know you're going to use one day. There's something like 2.3 billion square feet of rentable self-storage space in the United States, which means we often have so much stuff that we don't have room for it. If you've spent any time in the church, you know that following Jesus is a life centered on simplicity. Our Lord didn't have a coin in his pocket when asked about taxes, didn't own a home when threatened by Herod, and seemed always to be on the move, teaching his followers not to worry about what you will wear or eat, because God will provide.

Jesus taught about money more often than we might care to admit. Eleven of Jesus's thirty-nine parables are about money, and if we took the time to do the numbers, one out of every seven verses in Luke's Gospel has something to do with money. Jesus also taught that we shouldn't worry about tomorrow (Matthew 6:34), should sell all that we own and give to the poor (Matthew 19:21), and called for people of faith to give to Caesar what is Caesar's and to give to God what is God's (Matthew 22:21).

It seems that Jesus wants to change our focus from what to collect or not to collect and turn our hearts toward what we truly treasure.

I'm not exactly sure what Jesus meant when he asked us to collect treasure for ourselves in heaven, but my hunch is that the treasure to which Jesus refers has more to do with memories and fulfilled promises than the items in our closet. In other words, it seems that Jesus wants to change our focus from what to collect or not to collect and turn our hearts toward what we truly treasure. I treasure seeing my son share a new funny face just before bedtime. I treasure experiencing the first moment when Scripture makes sense in a new Christian's life. I treasure the humbling and amazing calling of being a pastor. Of course, my son having a bedroom, having a place to hold Bible study, and having a car to get me to and from the church all play a role in experiencing these treasures, but they aren't the treasure itself.

Did the wise men's gifts have some kind of effect on how Jesus understood the role of treasure in our life? It's hard to say. Late in Jesus's life, when Mary anointed Jesus's feet with expensive perfume, he neither dismissed her nor encouraged the other disciples to follow suit. When Judas became perturbed with what he assumed to be a waste, Jesus replies, "Leave her alone. This perfume was to be used in preparation for my burial, and this is how she has used it. You always have the poor among you, but you won't always have me" (John 12:7-8).

Maybe the real mystery of these treasures that bookend Jesus's earthly life is that they unapologetically point to Jesus's death. Myrrh from the wise men and nard from Mary. It isn't about the treasures themselves, but what they mean. Why do we offer gifts this time of year? Are these gifts a means of thanksgiving? Are the gifts we share a means of making sure all around us have what they need? Maybe the gifts we wrap and place under the tree have more to do with our own affluence and need to be accepted and desired?

When the Grinch takes the Whos' presents, food, and decorations, he isn't motivated by greed. He doesn't have a personal problem with hoarding earthly treasure. But within the story, his actions do call attention to the temporary nature of earthly things. He is the thief who breaks in to steal. Had the Whos placed their trust and hung their whole Christmas celebration on these things, Christmas would indeed have been stopped from coming. But as they sing on Christmas morning, surprising the

Grinch on the top of the mountain, they demonstrate the value of heavenly treasure, which no thief can take away and no earthly threats can destroy.

If the Grinch wasn't motivated by greed when he stole the Whos' Christmas presents, food, and decorations, what was his purpose in doing so?

Do you collect anything, or know someone who does? If so, what is significant or special about the items you or they collect?

What do you think Jesus meant by "treasures in heaven"? What can you do to store up heavenly treasure for yourself?

WHEN YOU'RE SURE YOU'RE RIGHT

The Grinch stands at the precipice of Mt. Crumpit with a sleigh full of all the Whos' holiday fare. His sleigh teeters on the edge, ready to disappear into the abyss along with the Whos' hopes of a merry Christmas. The Grinch doesn't steal away Christmas for personal gain, power, or influence. At worst, it seems that he's causing harm for the sake of causing harm. It's like Saint Augustine who in the *Confessions* described his feelings about stealing pears from a neighbor's tree: "I was in love with my own ruin...not with the thing for which I was falling into decay, but with decay

MORE MAX!

The average time it takes to read *How the Grinch Stole Christmas!* aloud is about twelve minutes. In order to fill the television special time slot, the length of the story had to double. Geisel was concerned about the story feeling artificially padded, so when Chuck Jones, coproducer with Geisel, suggested they spend much of the extra story time needed by focusing on the Grinch's dog, Max, Geisel eagerly agreed, describing Max as "both observer and victim, at one with the audience…[an] Everydog—all love and limpness and loyalty."[2] Incidental music and songs fill the remaining time needed for the 30-minute special.

itself."[3] He wasn't hungry. He didn't want the pears in order to sell them at the market. He was in love with the act of stealing itself. It's true that the Grinch is bent on punishing the Whos for their love of Christmas, but does his dastardly deed go deeper? With a heart two sizes too small, why would we expect anything less than a love for wrongdoing? Regardless of his motivation, as he's pushing Christmas off the edge of a cliff, he cups his ear to hear the Whos' weeping, wailing, and gnashing of teeth. He's convinced that what he's done has worked. He is certain that his assumptions are right.

It's true that the Grinch is bent on punishing the Whos for their love of Christmas, but does his dastardly deed go deeper?

Google is my father's nemesis. Before we carried tiny computers in our pockets with the wealth of human knowledge at our fingertips, my dad was a walking search engine. There was no trivia question too tricky. With the rare exception of the occasional "I don't know," an answer he's never been ashamed to convey, my dad had a working knowledge of just about everything. One Sunday afternoon while watching the New Orleans Saints play the San Francisco 49ers, my father left the den to refill the chips and salsa. While he was away the announcer mentioned that Steve Young, the current quarterback of the 49ers, had gotten his NFL start with the Tampa Bay Buccaneers. When my dad returned I was so excited to share with him the new trivia factoid that I had learned. "Dad, did you know that Steve Young got his NFL start with Tampa Bay?" My dad paused for a moment, undoubtedly searching his mind palace to either confirm or deny this new bit of information.

After a moment his lips started pursing, eyes began to squint, and his head started leaning slightly to the right. We knew at that point that Dad's mind palace was coming up empty. He said, "I don't think that's right." I told him that I had just heard the announcer mention it while he was refilling the snacks. He still didn't believe me. Several minutes later the announcer again mentioned how Steve Young got his NFL start as a Buccaneer, but this time my dad was in the room to hear it. I looked back at him with an "I told you so, but I'm not going to say it, but I'm feeling it with every fiber of my being" kind of expression. Now, anytime someone in my family starts to purse their lips, squint their eyes, and cock their head to the side questioning whether or not something is true, we call it "Steve Young Face." Of course, having a search engine in one's pocket, it is a dangerous affair to meet a fun fact with "Steve Young Face," which is why my father will never live this moment down.

Sometimes we just know we are right. In fact, I've never met someone who didn't agree with his or her own position or opinion. The Grinch is sure that he will be successful in his attempt to ruin the Whos' Christmas. He momentarily stops pushing the gifts off the mountaintop in order to hear the lamenting wails he is sure are about to radiate from the town below. I wonder if Herod opened the palace windows to hear the faint wailing all the way from Bethlehem.

*When Herod saw that he had been tricked by the
wise men, he was infuriated, and he sent and killed
all the children in and around Bethlehem who were
two years old or under, according to the time that he
had learned from the wise men. Then was fulfilled
what had been spoken through the prophet Jeremiah:*

"A voice was heard in Ramah,
  wailing and loud lamentation,
Rachel weeping for her children;
    she refused to be consoled, because they are no more."
                (Matthew 2:16-18 NRSV)

Herod was convinced he was doing the right thing to pre-
serve his power and influence over the Jewish people. The very
next verse in the story begins with, "When Herod died…" It's
a poignant statement of how poisonous our thirst for power can
become, especially if we confuse earthly influence with eternal
life. Not even Herod in all his efforts can escape the inevitable.
His murderous rampage may have temporarily secured the throne,
but this stark neighboring verse unveils how barren our quest for
power becomes. This prophecy from Jeremiah is one I wish had
gone unfulfilled, but it reveals that it's relatively easy to imagine a
future full of sorrow.

But there's something startling in the Grinch's story. His curious listening momentarily stops his awful idea. As he intently listens for the disappointed Whos, he forgets to nudge the gifts over
the mountain's edge. It's like the stereotypical villain in a hero's
story. It appears that the villain has won, but just before pressing

93

the big red button to destroy the world, he details his entire plan to the main character, and then he has the audacity to be shocked when his plan is eventually foiled. The Grinch's own sureness of success leads to his own failure to erase any sign of Christmas. Or could it be that somewhere, deep down in his small heart, he's unknowingly looking for a reason not to follow through? It reminds me of when Abraham was climbing Mount Moriah to offer his son Isaac as a sacrifice to the Lord. I imagine that as he lifts the knife into the air, he is praying for there to be some kind of sign or revelation to stop him from doing the unthinkable. After all, before he traveled up the mountain he told his servants, "the boy and I will walk up there, worship, and then come back to you" (Genesis 22:5). Thankfully in Abraham's case, an angel of the Lord did swoop in to stay the knife. Could it be that Abraham tarried just long enough for divine intervention to take place?

Could it be that God is at work even in the Grinches of our lives, even in the Grinch within each of us?

Maybe this is why we wait during the season of Advent. We pause and ponder the mystery that is about to take place. In our silent and pensive waiting, we make room for certain prophecies to go unfulfilled. We take the time to reconsider, or maybe weigh for the first time, the magnitude of what it means for God to take on flesh and become vulnerable in our selfish and power-hungry world. Could it be that God is at work even in the Grinches of our lives, even in the Grinch within each of us? When they wait just long enough to validate their own justification, they leave room for the Holy Spirit to keep the toys on the cliff's edge, the gifts that will eventually become the vehicle through which they find peace and reconciliation.

What assumptions did the Grinch make when he came up with this his "wonderful, awful idea"? Which of these assumptions proved true, and which did not?

Why did the Grinch pause at the top of the mountain before flinging the Whos' possessions off the cliff? Was it just to savor his success, or do you think there was something else behind it?

What is the role of waiting in the season of Advent? What do we hope will happen as we pause for a moment and ponder what God is doing?

THE MANGER OF LOVE

We must be at peace with ourself, our neighbor, and our God. This peace offers a framework through which our holy imaginations can envision a godly hope, a hope that begins to blur the lines that we like to draw in the world, but then love...love begins to turn things upside down. Have you seen *Frozen 2*? You should. There is a great song that Queen Elsa sings called "Into the Unknown." One of the things I most love about the song is the driving orchestration that makes the song sound like it's constantly on the move. I think most of us might add a question mark in the title—"Into the Unknown?"—and the orchestra for us might not be as gracious in its tempo and drive. At least for me the music would be much more tentative as I hesitate at the threshold of the unknown. Queen Elsa, however, sings it with boldness as if she can't wait to step out and experience whatever lies in store.

The third week of Advent offers us the grace and space to ponder Mary, Jesus's mother. Mary is thrust into the unknown, not unknown in the sense that she wasn't aware of what was being asked of her; rather, as is often the case with love, Mary is given few guarantees. I often chuckle when I hear the song "Mary Did You Know?" Mary, did you know? Yes! Mary knew a great number of things after she was visited by the angel Gabriel. Of course, she didn't know everything, which is a testament to her faithful response to what God was calling her to do. This journey into the relative unknown happens in three scenes: Annunciation, Affirmation, and Proclamation.

In the first scene, Annunciation, Mary is presented as a prophet in God's story.

> *In the sixth month the angel Gabriel was sent by God to a town in Galilee called Nazareth, to a virgin engaged to a man whose name was Joseph, of the house of David. The virgin's name was Mary. And he came to her and said, "Greetings, favored one! The Lord is with you." But she was much perplexed by his words and pondered what sort of greeting this might*

96

be. The angel said to her, "Do not be afraid, Mary,
for you have found favor with God. And now, you
will conceive in your womb and bear a son, and you
will name him Jesus. He will be great, and will be
called the Son of the Most High, and the Lord God
will give to him the throne of his ancestor David.
He will reign over the house of Jacob forever, and of
his kingdom there will be no end." Mary said to the
angel, "How can this be, since I am a virgin?" The
angel said to her, "The Holy Spirit will come upon
you, and the power of the Most High will overshadow
you; therefore the child to be born will be holy; he
will be called Son of God. And now, your relative
Elizabeth in her old age has also conceived a son;
and this is the sixth month for her who was said to
be barren. For nothing will be impossible with God."
Then Mary said, "Here am I, the servant of the Lord;
let it be with me according to your word." Then the
angel departed from her.

(Luke 1:26-38 NRSV)

Understand that when an angel says, "You have found favor
with God," it does not mean wealth, prosperity, and the easy life.
Mary, like the other prophets, is called to offer God's word, but
unlike the other prophets, this calling asks for Mary to offer her
entire self. Even today pregnancy can be dangerous. In the ancient
world, mothers often quite literally gave their life for the child's.
Mary was given no guarantees.

In the second scene she travels from the hill country in the
north to meet with Elizabeth in the south, and when she arrives,

she finds that what the angel said about Elizabeth was true. There is Affirmation, but this affirmation doesn't solely rest with knowing that Elizabeth is pregnant. God is doing something remarkable in the background that we must understand. Israel had been a divided kingdom—Israel in the north and Judea in the south. When Mary and Elizabeth meet, it is a sign that God is uniting a divided people. Theologically, the kingdom is being restored. Not only that, Elizabeth is married to Zechariah, a priest and keeper of the law. Mary, as we have seen, is being presented as a prophet in her own right. So, not only is the meeting of Mary and Elizabeth a unification of the old kingdom, it is a coming together of the Law and the Prophets. Not only that, but God is doing this through two women who had no children. In the ancient world a woman's value was centered on her ability to bear children. Elizabeth was old and thought to be barren. Mary was not yet married and was a virgin. Yet through these two women and their miraculous children, God is unifying the kingdom, uniting the Law and the Prophets, and bringing hope for God's people into the world.

In this third scene, Proclamation, Mary offers a prophetic word commonly known as The Magnificat.

> *He has brought down the powerful from their thrones,*
> *and lifted up the lowly;*
> *he has filled the hungry with good things,*
> *and sent the rich away empty.*
> *(Luke 1:52-53 NRSV)*

Mary did you know? Yes! But what Mary didn't know is what was in store for her. The angel said that she would be overshadowed by God, but how dark would the shadow be? When Mary and Joseph present Jesus in the Temple eight days after he is born, the prophet Simeon says, "This boy is assigned to be the cause of the falling and rising of many in Israel and to be a sign that generates opposition so that the inner thoughts of many will be revealed. And a sword will pierce your innermost being too" (Luke 2:34-35). Recently one of my church members wrote a beautiful reflection on the day before her son left to join the Marines, saying, "Our job as parents is definitely not an easy one.... He has nine months before he leaves for basic, which is kind of fitting. I had nine months to get ready for him to arrive, and now I have nine months to get ready for him to leave."

Love doesn't mean that everything will work out the way we plan. Love doesn't mean that there won't be suffering, hardship, or guarantees of the "good life"; but love never tires of making sure that we are valued and that we are precious and that we are God's own.

Annunciation, Affirmation, and Proclamation. Mary was moving into the unknown indeed, not because she didn't know who Jesus was or would be; rather she was given very little guarantee about herself, and she said yes to God anyway. That's the thing about love, isn't it? Love doesn't mean that everything will work out the way we plan. Love doesn't mean that there won't be suffering, hardship, or guarantees of the "good life"; but love never tires of making sure that we are valued and that we are precious and that we are God's own. Peace helps us build a framework so that we have the holy imagination to hope for a better tomorrow, but love is disarming. Love is the dismantling. Love believes all things and bears all things. Love never ends. "How can this be?" Mary asked. Because nothing is impossible with God.

Think about Gabriel's message to Mary. What did she know after the angel spoke, and what remained unknown?

When have you followed God's call on an unknown path? What did you find as you ventured forth?

Can there ever be any guarantees in love? Why or why not?

CHAPTER FOUR

WHEN JOY IS OUR SONG

So, here we are. The Grinch has succeeded. None of the Whos have any presents or decorations or even food for Christmas Day. The Grinch is sure that his wonderful, awful idea worked, and he has every reason to believe that it had. He has this image in his mind that all of the Whos would wake up, and their mouths would be open for a minute or two before they begin weeping and wailing as they notice what had happened. Well, the Whos mouths were open early in the morning, but they weren't weeping and wailing; rather they began to sing. What happened? Why were they not wailing? We might understand a melody of lament or a rallying cry encouraging the Whos to storm the mountain, but the music the Grinch heard led to his heart growing three sizes. How could this be? If you want to talk about the vehicle through which a heart can grow three sizes, music is the perfect example.

Music is unparalleled in its ability to move us, to illicit a response within us. It's almost subconscious.

Music is unparalleled in its ability to move us, to illicit a response within us. It's almost subconscious. When we hear a song in a major key, our bodies involuntarily respond with happiness. Similarly, when we hear music in a minor key we "feel" sadness. It's as if there's a fundamental connection between us and music, and that actually makes great sense. One prominent scientific theory about the fundamental nature of matter is called "String Theory." The idea of String Theory is that matter, everything that is, is the result of tiny vibrating strings, and the frequency of the different vibrations is how we get different particles. Those particles, like quarks, then make up larger particles like protons, which constitute atoms, which make up, well, everything, including you and me. Vibrations moving through the air is what music is, so for a moment consider that you are a song. We are a part of God's grand orchestra, and our role is to be in harmony with the music of the spheres, so to speak. Of course, not everything is in harmony. There is discord, and there is tension. Sometimes it's hard to hear God's melody with all of the noise about.

That is where the Grinch was. At the beginning of the story, he's standing outside his miserable home, and the music he hears coming from Whoville sounds like noise to him. It's aggravating and intense. It's like when the apostle Paul says in 1 Corinthians, "[If] I don't have love, I am a clanging gong or a clashing cymbal" (13:1). In other words, when our heart is two sizes too small it almost doesn't matter what the song is. We can't hear it well. When the ancient Israelites were in captivity in Egypt and Pharaoh's heart was hardened, I have a feeling that there wasn't much singing. But when God's people finally find themselves on the other side of the Red Sea, Miriam, with tambourine in hand, sings, "Sing to the LORD, for an overflowing victory!" (Exodus 15:21). WhenMary meets Elizabeth, they are both pregnant. Mary breaks out in song, "With all my heart I glorify the Lord! / In the depths of who I am I rejoice in God my savior" (Luke 1:46-47). Throughout Scripture, in moments of celebration and liberation we find music.

It is no surprise to me that the Advent and Christmas season is saturated with music, music that defies denominational boundary, music that isn't only played on Christian radio stations, music that can be heard in marketplaces and festivals and theme parks. It's everywhere. How is it even possible to talk about angels in the sky without singing, "Gloria, in excelsis deo!" Can you imagine what Christmas would be like if we weren't singing? Maybe you don't have to imagine it. During the COVID-19 pandemic we suspended congregational singing in our sanctuary, as many other churches did. It was a difficult but necessary decision.

In that difficult season, it was obvious that something was terribly missing from our worship. Admittedly, I am biased. For most of my undergraduate career, my major was vocal performance. Although it is charming that Buddy the Elf thinks singing is just talking really loudly, singing involves the entire body. Your eyes have to make sense of the notes, lines, and spaces; your mind has to keep track of rhythm and dynamics; you have to breathe energetically while keeping your body relaxed; your ears have to mark the correct key; and then finally when all of these things come together, you open your mouth to produce sound, never mind the art of interpreting what the composer is meaning to communicate. The act of standing and singing in worship involves the whole self, and without it worship can sometimes feel like taking your first bite of a hamburger just after everything slips out from between the buns.

But when [the Grinch] listens, he hears singing. He's heard the Whos sing before, and it was noise to him; but this time it stirs his soul, and it makes his heart tremble.

Something was terribly missing from the Grinch as well. He stands on the mountaintop listening for the lamentations that he knew would follow when the Whos discovered his wonderful, awful idea. But when he listens, he hears singing. He's heard the Whos sing before, and it was noise to him; but this time it stirs his soul, and it makes his heart tremble. Why? What song could they possibly sing that would be so powerful to even transform the heart of the Grinch?

In the television special, the Whos sing a song called "Welcome Christmas" that Dr. Seuss wrote for the show. But the original book doesn't tell us the name of the song or its lyrics. It simply says that the Whos were singing, leaving us to imagine what the song may have been. I like to picture the Whos singing something like this:

> My life flows on in endless song
> Above earth's lamentation
> I hear the clear, though far-off hymn
> That hails a new creation
>
> Through all the tumult and the strife
> I hear that music ringing
> It finds an echo in my soul
> How can I keep from singing?
>
> No storm can shake my inmost calm
> While to that Rock I'm clinging
> Since love is Lord of heaven and earth
> How can I keep from singing?[1]

We don't know what the Whos sang, but we should rightly imagine that it wasn't a sweet Christmas carol about reindeer or snow. It was probably a song that spoke a deep and profound truth, a song that you can't help but sing when you wake up to find that everything you have is gone. "Since love is Lord of heaven and earth, how can I keep from singing?" Through their song the Grinch discovers that Christmas isn't about the packages or presents or decorations. It is about love, a love that we celebrate in the best of time, and a love we cling to in times of strife and oppression. Jesus is what God's love looks like, and that's what Christmas is about. Finally recognizing this truth is what caused the Grinch's heart to grow. How could it not?

What is your favorite Christmas song? How does it make you feel?

Why is music so central to our observance of Christmas?

THE HEART THAT GREW THREE SIZES

We don't know why the Grinch's heart grew three sizes, but I like to think that it grew once for each of the scenes we see in Luke's record of Jesus's birth. In the first scene the curtain opens and we see a magnificent palace, the seat of human power and authority. Caesar has the authority to order the lives of seemingly the entire world, or at least the world that mattered enough to be counted. The news of Caesar's census travels to Quirinius, governor of Syria, who enjoys a lower status than does Ceasar, but he is important enough to be forever remembered by name. Joseph and Mary enter the scene preparing to make the journey from Nazareth in the north to Bethlehem in the south so that the proper authorities may count them. While they were there in Bethlehem, the "city of bread," the time came for Mary to deliver her child. She gave birth to a baby boy, wrapped him snugly, and placed him in a manger because there was no room for them in the inn.

The scene begins in the palace, the seat of all authority. The Grinch at the beginning of the story seems to think he holds a similar power. Instead of ordering the world to temporarily move to their ancestral home, he goes to their homes in the hope of moving them to despair. Instead of counting the people so that he could record their possessions, he takes their possessions to elicit misery. Though the actions of Caesar and the Grinch were different, their hunger for power is quite the same. Both wanted their respective worlds to know who was in charge. The Grinch's growing heart is so much more than a sentimental warm fuzzy. Hearing the Whos sing a joyful tune is like a peasant from Judea saying "No" to Caesar's order. I would imagine that defying Caesar's census would be met with a growing legion of soldiers rather than a growing heart. The Grinch's transformation is remarkable. Instead of growing even more embittered by his own failure, he becomes more malleable. The sweet sound of singing disarms him. In this first scene of the Christmas story we are also unexpectedly disarmed. Through Luke's careful unfolding from Caesar to Christ, we begin to realize that it is the child in the manger, and not the emperor in the palace, who has the power to move us. As the first scene concludes, the Grinch's heart has grown by one size.

In the second scene we find ourselves outside Bethlehem where shepherds keep a watchful eye over their flock, peering into the darkness for any signs of danger. Then an angel of the Lord stood before them, and they were afraid. Their job was to protect the herd from danger, and now standing before them is a frightful and unfamiliar sight. It is no surprise that the angel quickly calls

SMART INVESTING

When the storyboards were completed for the Grinch television special, Chuck Jones, head of MGM Animation, began shopping the project around to different investors and producers. After being rejected by twenty-six different potential sponsors, Jones finally received an investment from the Foundation for Commercial Banks, to which Jones replied, "You have to be kidding.... The bankers bought a story in which the Grinch says 'maybe Christmas doesn't come from a store'??!! Well, bless their banker hearts!"[2]

out to them saying, "Don't be afraid." I would imagine even after the angel heralds them with peace, their grip on their staves and rods tightened. Then, the angel says something curious: "This is a sign for you: you will find a newborn baby wrapped snugly and lying in a manger" (Luke 2:12).

Scripture doesn't say that the shepherds were looking for a sign, or that they were particularly interested in searching for anything beyond what would get their herd through the night. Nevertheless, the angel says, "You *will* find." It's so definitive. It almost sounds like a command, and it's hard to blame the shepherds if they thought it was. It was more the case, as my friend James Howell reminded me, "You may want to poke your head around to see what's happening in your own neighborhood. Aren't you interested in a bit of a 'child-like' surprise from heaven?"

It's not that Christmas is bigger and better, or the latest and greatest. Christmas simply is more.

The Grinch, too, was in for a bit of a surprise. For the shepherds, finding a child wrapped snugly was not the gift that they had expected, nor was it something for which they were searching. In the same way, the Grinch came to an unexpected realization. The singing he heard was so disarming that it caused him to stop for three hours to reconsider everything. Christmas came anyway. Christmas didn't depend on gifts under the tree, figgy pudding on the table, or stockings hung by the fireplace with care. In short, he realized that Christmas was more. It's not that Christmas is bigger and better, or the latest and greatest. Christmas simply is more.

Christmas is abundant. Christmas is our human cup running over with divine favor and grace. Christmas is more than denominational lines. Christmas is more than our petty divisions and Twitter squabbles. Christmas is more than our traditions, hymns, candles, and wreaths. Take everything away, and Jesus was born anyway, and continues to be born within us through God's grace every day. Love truly did "come down" at Christmas. Psalm 136 reads as if we are hearing God's heartbeat.

> *O give thanks to the LORD, for he is good,*
> *for his steadfast love endures forever.*
> *O give thanks to the God of gods,*
> *for his steadfast love endures forever.*
> *O give thanks to the Lord of lords,*
> *for his steadfast love endures forever.*
> *(Psalm 136:1-3 NRSV)*

And on and on it goes—"his steadfast love endures forever...his steadfast love endures forever..." The singing caused his heart to grow one size, and now, with his realization that Christmas is more, the Grinch's heart has grown two sizes.

Take everything away and Christmas remains, and fortunately the Grinch still has everything he stole. Though his sleigh is teetering on the edge of a cliff, it has not yet fallen. He pulls everything back from the brink and decides to go, with haste, down the mountain to return the Christmas he tried to devour.

As the curtain opens on scene three of the Christmas story, the shepherds say, "Let us go now to Bethlehem and see this thing that has taken place, which the Lord has made known to us" (Luke 2:15b). The Grinch and shepherds alike are filled with a sense of urgency. It reminds me of my young son, Robert, who on Christmas morning wants to play with all of his gifts immediately after they've been opened. "Daddy, can you open this?" is a constant refrain.

The shepherds finally make their way to the Holy Family and when they see the Christ Child, they tell everyone everything that had happened, like a child who darts out of the living room before breakfast to show the next-door neighbor what Santa left under the tree. When we approach this Word, the place where the seemingly parallel lines of the human and the divine intersect, I don't know whether I would kneel in adoration or keep my distance out of awe or reverence, but at least I know that I would leave changed. The Grinch charges down the mountain and returns everything that he packed away in the middle of the night. This act of giving, though he shouldn't have stolen it in the first place, is when his heart finally grows a third size. We often hear that giving is better than receiving, and for the Grinch, this is certainly true.

The Christmas story is a three-scene play that leads us from the palace to the manger, bringing us closer to God's own incarnate heart. We find in the Grinch's story a three-part transformation of his own heart, which started out two sizes too small and grew to the point of overflowing. His heart had been transformed, and it was transformed yet again when he rushed to share the fruits of that change with everyone else.

How does the Grinch respond when he first hears the Whos singing? What does this say about his heart in that moment?

For most of us, the Christmas story is a familiar one. Read it again, slowly, with fresh eyes in Luke chapter 2. Is there anything surprising about it? If so, what?

Is the Grinch's decision to return the Whos' possession a cause or an effect of his transformation? Why?

PEACE WITH JUSTICE

The story isn't over. How would the Whos react to this radically redeemed outsider whose heart seemed to miraculously grow three sizes larger? I certainly wouldn't blame them if they were suspicious of the Grinch's newfound grace. The Whos seem perfectly in the right should they want to bring the Grinch to justice. If the story were told today, I fear that the Grinch wouldn't have made it out of the first house alive. After all, he did sneak into all their homes and steal their possessions. It's a common enough story in our society for people to shoot first and ask questions later when possessions are threatened. How tragic and empty the ending of that story would be. It seems that the Whos have the final say in how this story will end.

Last words seem heavier than other thoughts we share. I dread thinking about what my last words are going to be. I hope that I say something profound like, "Best of all, God is with us," like John Wesley, or Steve Jobs's famous, "Oh wow!" Undoubtedly, it's more likely that I'll utter, "Check this out," as I recklessly tumble off a hover board forgetting that I'm no longer a teenager, or something dangerously mundane like, "That's not a poisonous snake."

Have you ever considered what your last words might be, or at least how you might want to be remembered? Of course, the tricky thing about last words is that rarely do we know that last words will be last words, which begs the question why all of our words aren't treated with the same emphasis, dignity, and importance. I've always found it curious that traditionally we attribute Jesus's last words as being things he said from the cross like, "Father forgive them," or "Today you will be with me in Paradise," or "My God, why have you forsaken me." Never mind that saying anything from the cross is exceedingly difficult, but we like these last words. They are comforting, and they are profound, but they aren't challenging. Maybe that's why the church likes them so much—because they aren't asking anything of us.

In Luke's Gospel Jesus's last words are a summary of who the Messiah is, and what is required of us as followers: "This is what is written: the Christ will suffer and rise from the dead on the third day, and a change of heart and life for the forgiveness of sins must be preached in his name to all nations, beginning from Jerusalem. You are witnesses of these things" (24:46-48). It seems that when Jesus's earthly ministry was over, Jesus wanted the disciples to remember forgiveness above all else.

113

We are charged to forgive while we hope for reconciliation. Reconciliation follows forgiveness, and sometimes forgiveness takes a long time.

Forgiveness is refusing your right to harm someone in the way that she or he has harmed you. Forgiveness isn't necessarily rebuilding friendship or bringing a relationship back to what it was. Another way to say this is that we are charged to forgive while we hope for reconciliation. Reconciliation follows forgiveness, and sometimes forgiveness takes a long time. How many times must we forgive our neighbor? Seventy times seven times, Jesus said, which is another way to say, you might have to do it every day for a good long while. Forgiveness doesn't mean that you are a doormat; rather forgiveness is freedom. It means that you are no longer bound by your anger and frustration toward someone else. I love how Paul puts it in Romans 12:

> *Do not repay anyone evil for evil, but take thought for what is noble in the sight of all. If it is possible, so far as it depends on you, live peaceably with all. Beloved, never avenge yourselves, but leave room for the wrath of God; for it is written, "Vengeance is mine, I will repay, says the Lord." No, "if your enemies are hungry, feed them; if they are thirsty, give them something to drink; for by doing this you will heap burning coals on their heads." Do not be overcome by evil, but overcome evil with good.*
> *(12:17-21 NRSV)*

I love the honesty of that. Leave room for the wrath of God, not your own wrath. Forgiveness is hard work, especially when we realize that often the person we have to forgive is ourself.

In the musical *Hamilton*, there is a beautiful song near the end of the musical titled "It's Quiet Uptown." At this point in Alexander Hamilton's story, he has been unfaithful to his wife, he has lost his oldest son in a reckless duel, and he's lost nearly all of his political influence. He hasn't yet lost his relationship with his wife, Eliza, but she has every reason in the world to separate herself from Alexander's recklessness and irresponsibility.

In lieu of analyzing the entire song in the context of the musical, I want to point out where the song begins and ends. As Eliza and Alexander wrestle with infidelity and the loss of their son, the song begins with:

> There are moments that the words don't reach
> There is suffering too terrible to name

Alexander has spent a lifetime using words to sort out his influence, struggle, and objectives, but now, words fall flat and useless. There are moments that the words don't reach. The music is slow, pointed, and meaningful; quite the opposite of most of the musical's fast-paced excitement. What the couple is now experiencing is completely counter to what is familiar, expected, and knowable. By the end of the song, after Alexander has reflected on his role in tearing his family apart, wrestling with his own lowliness, and his acceptance of his own unworthiness to be a husband and a father, you hear:

THE PERFECT ENDING

The most hotly debated production piece for the Grinch animated television special was how to craft the ending. Geisel was adamant about not making the ending either too preachy or too saccharine. Maurice Noble, the background artist, stepped in and suggested that the Whos should join hands creating the symbol of a star, and then the "star moved up and joined with the Grinch, and he was transformed," to which Geisel responded, "Perfect!"[3] Although several critics panned the special saying it "fell a trifle short of expectation,"[4] the Grinch television special would become one of the most beloved Christmas classics even to this day.

There are moments that the words don't reach
There's a grace too powerful to name...
Forgiveness...can you imagine?

It's heart-wrenching. It's both real and truly unimaginable. Forgiveness is truly a grace too powerful to name...and it is also our calling as followers of Christ. Jesus's last words to the disciples were, "forgiveness must be preached in [my] name," and the Whos seem to have taken this to heart.

What led the Whos to receive and welcome the Grinch? Would you have done the same thing if you were in their shoes? Why or why not?

Recall a time when you experienced the power of forgiveness.

What does it mean that the Whos, not the Grinch, ultimately decide how the story ends? What does this say about the way we practice forgiveness in our lives?

AT THE TABLE

At the end of *How the Grinch Stole Christmas!* we see that the Grinch, the outsider, the other, the one who should be feared and excluded, was the one who is now at the head of the table, carving the roast beast, as they all sit together in table fellowship.

Not only does it seem that all things are forgiven, but the Whos have given the Grinch a seat of honor! The last panel of Seuss's story has a wreath behind the Grinch as he carves the roast beast, and it almost looks like a halo. The Gospel isn't explicit in Seuss's story, but this simple final drawing reveals something holy has been experienced. Something beautiful has taken place, and how perfect it is that enemies are now around the same table sharing a meal, with the least of these at the head of the table. We mistakenly think that the point of Seuss's story is that Christmas isn't about presents. The true insight of this story is the joy of reconciliation.

Joy is the steadfast assurance that God is with us. God is with us yesterday, today, and tomorrow. One of the most profound things about our Advent discipline is peace, hope, love, and joy's relationship with time. Advent is a season when we prepare for something that's already happened. One of the things that I love about Christianity is its complete and appropriate disregard of linear time. For example, folks have asked me, "If Jesus died and was raised in roundabout AD 33, what about the people who died in AD 32? Were they just out of luck?" No. Paul says that God was pleased to reconcile all things through Christ. The experience of time is part of creation. Time is simply God's way of making sure everything doesn't happen at once.

All things were reconciled. Time is part of that "all." The cross works both forward and backward. When we gather around the Communion table, our faith reveals that we gather with the saints and the heavenly host. Why was Jesus born when he was? Scripture says, "When the fulfillment of the time came, God sent his Son, born through a woman, and born under the Law" (Galatians 4:4). Jesus was born when time was full. Time itself needed to be unburdened. This points to the mystery of joy; joy is timeless. Chris Wiman edited a fantastic book of poems on joy, and I love what he wrote in the introduction: "To define joy as present tense is to keep it fastened to time, and that doesn't feel completely right. It might be truer to say that joy is a flash of eternity that *illuminates* time, but the word 'eternity' does sit a bit lumpishly there on the page."[5]

Love is an expression of the past....
Peace is our work in the present....
Hope projects us into the future....
Joy in its timelessness brings
all three together at once.

Joy is a "flash of eternity," and when placed in the context of our Advent discipline, it makes perfect sense. Love is an expression of the past. We gather because of God's love in the person of Jesus two thousand years ago. Peace is our work in the present. Putting down the sword and working toward reconciliation. Hope projects us into the future, ultimately when there will be a new heaven and a new earth. Joy in its timelessness brings all three together at once. Peace, hope, and love, the past, present, and future, all proclaiming that Father, Son, and Holy Spirit is always with us—eternal joy.

Advent is not a time of waiting for gifts. Advent is a time of waiting to recognize that the Giver is the gift. The gift is the invitation into God's story. It is a story of how the human and the divine have come together in Christ and in the body of Christ, the church, and how through this union humans are empowered to love as God loves. Sam Wells says this beautifully:

> In earthly human friendship it is impossible to know everyone, still less to care or genuinely to love more than a limited number or range of people. Yet Jesus is the good shepherd, who knows all of his sheep and calls them each by name; he lays down his life for them. He is prepared to leave the great mass of them to seek and find just one. He has other sheep, "not of this fold," whom he knows just as well. . . . In other words, in the life of the kingdom it is possible to love all with the intensity with which one might aspire on earth to love one; and that love and attention do not disclose deep flaws but evoke profound awe.[6]

God is the gift, and the gift is an invitation to participate in God's story. Through Christ, God dwells within each of us. We are, the church is, the body of Christ, the place where God's story of love continues, the place where God's story of love is offered to the world. God is love, so when we learn to care, when we learn to share our gifts with the world, when we learn to seek out and welcome the lost sheep searching for truth, when we make room for those society has forgotten or have found unlovable—that is when we experience the very heart of God. When we do these things we create a place for God to dwell.

The Whos seem to understand this profound truth of the beauty of Christmas, even though their celebration seemed noisily hidden behind trinkets and treasures. At the end of it all both the Grinch and the Whos got it right. They both sat at the same table, gave the least of these the seat of honor, and though not explicitly, revealed the timeless truth that God is with us.

Why do you think Dr. Seuss chose a meal as the final scene of How the Grinch Stole Christmas!?

How does the promise of Christ, God with us, expand our own capacity to love?

THE ANGEL OF JOY

Peace offers the framework through which our holy imaginations can perceive a hope in which the revelation of love is disarming, convicting, and comforting. Joy, on the other hand, is wholly other. Peace is an artful, humble, and active intention. Hope is a destination toward which we strive. Love is something that must be given and received. Joy is not something we can do. Joy simply is found. Again, Chris Wiman puts it well, saying, "[Joy is] the place that is most us yet remains beyond us."[7]

Joy is not something we can do.
Joy simply is found.

"Don't be afraid! Look! I bring good news to you—wonderful, joyous news for all people. Your savior is born today in David's city. He is Christ the Lord," the angel announces (Luke 2:10-11). Two parallel lines, the human and the divine, coming together, in the place that is most us yet remains beyond us. It would take an angel to announce joy because I'm not sure we have the words to do it. We often think of joy as being happiness, but happiness is to joy as black and white is to color. Joy certainly isn't sadness, and yet there is a depth to a joyful experience that sometimes only sadness knows.

My wife, Christie, and I experienced joy earlier this year. I have rarely mentioned this publicly because we have been both embarrassed and ashamed, but I think it cuts to the heart of what Joy is. Earlier this year we took the family to Walt Disney World. One night the kids were swimming at the pool, and I brought back pizza for us to eat. Everyone got out of the pool, and we took our youngest child Robert's life jacket off so that he could sit at the table. We started mapping out what our next day was going to be. Eventually the kids finished their pizza and wanted to go back into the pool, so one by one they peeled away from the table as Christie and I kept talking. I'm not sure how long it was, but we heard Robert crying, his face was pale, and a woman named Amanda was holding him. Immediately we knew what had happened. We forgot to put his life jacket back on, and we didn't know how long he had been in the pool without it. She said that she saw him get in and she thought he was playing, but then realized that he wasn't as she scooped him out of the pool.

That night we felt a great joy. Amanda happened to be in the right place at the right time and all at once there was shock, embarrassment, grief over what if, and relief that everything was OK. It was like the soul exhaling. I don't tell you this to suggest that we were somehow favored by God in that moment. But I can say that every time I see that child smile, as the apostle Paul says in Romans 8, "the Spirit intercedes with sighs too deep for words" (Romans 8:26b NRSV).

Joy is the soul exhaling. "I bring good news to you—wonderful, joyous news" is all of creation taking in a breath and holding it until the baby Jesus breathes his first, and then all at once all of creation exhales and the greatest joy of all creation finds its place that is both within us and beyond us. Peace, the framework, hope, the vision, and love, the activity of God have all been pointing us to that intersecting line of the human and the divine that offers joy to the world, now and forever.

Joy is something we can't do or achieve; it's something we receive. How can you recognize joy when you have it?

How is reconciliation at the heart of Christmas? What can you do to make reconciliation a part of the way you celebrate Christmas this year?

NOTES

CHAPTER 1

1 Neil Morgan and Judith Giles Morgan, *Dr. Seuss and Mr. Geisel: A Biography* (New York: Da Capo Press, 1996), 157–158.

2 Brian Jay Jones, "How Dr. Seuss Stole Christmas: The Making of the Classic Grinch Holiday Cartoon" (saturdayeveningpost.com, November/December 2019), 37.

3 Stanley Hauerwas, *Matthew: Brazos Theological Commentary on the Bible* (Grand Rapids, MI: Brazos Press, 2006), 35.

4 Paraphrased from the film *The Lord of the Rings: The Return of the King.*

CHAPTER 2

1 Brian Jay Jones, 37.

2 Gian-Carlo Menotti, *Amahl and the Night Visitors* (RCA Victor LM-1701, 1962), 5–6.

CHAPTER 3

1   Brian Jay Jones, 36.
2   Brian Jay Jones, 36.
3   Augustine, *The Confessions* (New York: Vintage Books, 1997), 30.

CHAPTER 4

1   "My Life Flows On (How Can I Keep from Singing?)," words by Robert Lowry, *The Faith We Sing* (Nashville: Abingdon Press, 2000), 2212.
2   Brian Jay Jones, 36.
3   Brian Jay Jones, 38.
4   Brian Jay Jones 39.
5   Christian Wiman, ed., *Joy: 100 Poems* (New Haven, CT: Yale University Press, 2019), xiv.
6   Samuel Wells, *God's Companions: Reimagining Christian Ethics* (Oxford, UK: Wiley-Blackwell, 2006), 41.
7   Christian Wiman, xix.

Made in the USA
Middletown, DE
22 November 2023